Love and its Disappointment

The Meaning of Life,
Therapy and Art

First published by O Books, 2009
O Books is an imprint of John Hunt Publishing Ltd., The Bothy, Deershot Lodge, Park Lane, Ropley,
Hants, SO24 0BE, UK
office1@o-books.net
www.o-books.net

Distribution in:	South Africa
	Alternative Books
UK and Europe	altbook@peterhyde.co.za
Orca Book Services	Tel: 021 555 4027 Fax: 021 447 1430
orders@orcabookservices.co.uk	
Tel: 01202 665432 Fax: 01202 666219	Text copyright David Brazier 2008
Int. code (44)	
	Design: Stuart Davies
USA and Canada	
NBN	ISBN: 978 1 84694 209 9
custserv@nbnbooks.com	
Tel: 1 800 462 6420 Fax: 1 800 338 4550	All rights reserved. Except for brief quotations
	in critical articles or reviews, no part of this
Australia and New Zealand	book may be reproduced in any manner without
Brumby Books	prior written permission from the publishers.
sales@brumbybooks.com.au	
Tel: 61 3 9761 5535 Fax: 61 3 9761 7095	The rights of David Brazier as author have been
	asserted in accordance with the Copyright,
Far East (offices in Singapore, Thailand,	Designs and Patents Act 1988.
Hong Kong, Taiwan)	
Pansing Distribution Pte Ltd	
kemal@pansing.com	A CIP catalogue record for this book is available
Tel: 65 6319 9939 Fax: 65 6462 5761	from the British Library.

Printed by CPI Antony Rowe, Chippenham, Wiltshire

Love and its Disappointment

The Meaning of Life,
Therapy and Art

David Brazier

BOOKS

Winchester, UK
Washington, USA

CONTENTS

This book is dedicated to
Carl Ransom Rogers
Iris Murdoch &
Thomas Stearns Eliot

Part One:

The Theory in Context

Therapy, Love and Art

Psychotherapy is an art, art is therapeutic, and both therapy and art are forms of love. Love is the primary drive in human life. If we want to reduce all human functioning to a single drive we will not find a better or more useful one. Love finds its most immediate manifestation in a particular form of regard for which I shall use the term 'esteem' (in conscious contra-distinction to 'self-esteem' for reasons that shall become clear). Esteem refers to the manner in which love regards its object.

That said, in practice, all human functioning including activity, thought, emotion, imagination and so on, springs from and is enriched by conflicts of one sort or another, either among drives or between drives and existential factors. Life thus inevitably becomes a succession of essays at love encountering continual rebuff and frustration. Art (here including literature, poetry, plastic and visual arts, music, and other such expressions of high culture) and religion express this love-frustration chemistry and so act as a catalyst in the development of society. Therapy performs a similar task at the level of the individual.

Love involves courage and gives rise to a number of virtues that are situational rather than formulaic, such as honour, loyalty, duty, devotion, altruism and self-sacrifice. That these virtues have recently been regarded as outmoded may be symptomatic of how the balance of our lives has swung too far toward dependence upon codes, mechanisms and formulae and indicate a need to restore flexibility and humanity. Those involved in the practice of art, religion or therapy may, however, include both exemplars of such virtues and also those most lacking them: the people for whom such issues have become especially problematic, resolution most urgent.

Humans mediate these conflicts and try to maintain some predictability, continuity and reassuring stability in their lives by, largely unconsciously, constructing a sense of 'self' with its associated conceit (Brazier C. 2003). The notion of self allows the individual a measure of distance from a world that is often painful. The 'associated conceit' is the inevitable tendency to regard the self as more substantial than it in fact is, thus at least tingeing our interactions with fantasies of self-entitlement, self-justification, and self-imagery, together with no small measure of confusion, and sometimes leading us into gross distortions of perception: fantasies of omnipotence and, at the extreme, megalomania or madness.

Broadly, this picture is not offered in the spirit of a homily since there is no escape. We are inevitably, fundamentally loving beings and we are inevitably frustrated and this inevitably leads us also to be 'evil' in a variety of ways and this is what makes us 'characters'. I say 'evil' tentatively because definitions are contentious, but I mean to imply that we all end up doing unloving and harmful things as a result of being impelled by a drive toward love in a world that is as it is. We become twisted. This, therefore, is a theory of love, but also one about the inherent irony of existence. Therapy and art help us to develop as characters in a situation that inevitably has limits, problems and imperfections and to handle the reflections of these in ourselves yet with effects extending beyond ourselves.

In this volume my intention is not to elaborate extensively on the pathological, but to attempt to clarify the functioning of love in our lives, and particularly how an understanding of this functioning serves the purposes of the psychotherapist and the artist, as well as how that understanding can be widened and deepened by a comparison between the processes that occur in creativity and therapy. Therapy provides the major theme with, as a sub-plot, as it were, a theory of how the matter of love and its disappointment also provides a powerful explanatory principle in the arts and in cultural appreciation.

This approach of understanding life in terms of love and its disappointment is offered as an extension and elaboration of theory already set out in an earlier short work (Brazier D 1993b), and also as a means toward a degree of diminution in the technicalisation and esotericism of psychotherapy in particular and cultural appreciation in general. Thinking in terms of 'Love' provides a simpler and more direct vocabulary, in many instances. The varieties of self psychology that are currently popular in many quarters, though they work after a fashion, offer, on the whole, more convoluted explanations of common human phenomena.

The psychology developed here is 'other centred'. It rests upon the notion that our greatest satisfactions come through our esteem for others and our greatest frustrations through our conflicts with them; that our goal in life is not primarily self-perfection or self-actualisation, but satisfying relation to the world around us and ultimately the benefit of others (the species and the biosphere); that the all-to-widespread concern with self is a symptom of life over-distanced from its world. This implies that life is a constant negotiation, or, better, dance. It cannot have a self-sufficient goal either physically (for we are totally dependent upon 'outside' supplies of food, energy, etc.) or psychologically (for consciousness is always 'other regarding'). The goal of therapy is not that the client become an actualised self *unto him or herself*,[1] but a fully-functioning being-in-relation, ever changing and developing through the process of relating, not just to other people, but to all objects, which are, in practice, impermanent, and the optimum form of such relating is known to all as love.

As I wrote this work it became apparent that it would be easier to explain many points were we to have a term or terms for the theory here presented taken as a whole. The manner in which

3

I arrived at the theory, as will become clear below, owes a great deal to the seminal work of the American psychologist Carl Rogers. It seeks to resolve some of the remaining problems of his work. Once I had accepted that terminology was necessary it seemed natural to draw on his work with a variation that made the distinction of this work clear. After an initial phase in which his theory was called the 'non-directive method', Rogers adopted 'client centred therapy' as a rubric. I propose in this book to use the term 'other centred therapy' (OCT)[2] to emphasise both that the therapist in client-centred therapy is focussed upon the client, who is 'other' to him, and that what the client is trying to do is to make some progress in his or her regard for the 'others' in his own life. Later as Rogers developed his method extending it beyond the therapy situation (into education, for instance) he changed the name again to 'person-centred approach'. In similar spirit, when I am referring to the theory here presented in general terms that go beyond therapy, as in the arts, I shall call it the 'other-centred approach' (OCA). I shall also refer to this complex of ideas as 'esteem theory' from time to time, as much for stylistic reasons as any. OCA, or esteem theory, is a way of thinking about how our life is led by the manner in which we regard our love objects and OCT is the therapeutic application of such thinking. Later I shall also introduce a method called 'object related work' as one technical example of OCT.

Giving something a name is hazardous. I am uncomfortably conscious as I do so that setting up a name is always an invitation to abuse. I can only say that the terminology is a valuable utility within the purpose of this work. That it will be misused later is probably an unavoidable consequence that simply bears out the main thesis of this book: the road to Hell is paved with good intentions. By giving these principles a name one makes them into an 'other' and so something with which one can have a relationship. Sometimes that relationship may be one of love and esteem, but it will inevitably also lead todisappointment; such is the moral of this tale. However, it is my love of Rogers' approach and my frustration with it that has brought the matter thus far and I should not, therefore, complain too much when others take it further.

The book describes a closer association between therapy and the arts than is commonly asserted. This is not a new theme, having roots at least as early as Aristotle, to whom I shall have some important reference, yet it is a neglected one and one that seems worthy of reassertion since those who think about the human mind and those who think about society and its highest expressions have a good deal to learn from each other, especially now that therapy is no longer simply a means to restore people to 'normality' but has also become a road to better than normal levels of functioning. Therapy is frequently concerned with life enhancement beyond mere cure and, as we shall see later when reviewing Freud's treatment of 'Anna O', actually always has been. There is the possibility that by understanding the therapeutic effect of art we may better understand psychotherapy and also that by understanding the basic springs of the mind we shall be enabled to see more clearly what the artist is doing and why it matters to him or her to do it.

The term 'love' is often shied away from in theory texts and, no doubt, we risk misunderstanding by using it here. I think that the risk is worth running. It is important to re-establish what is important and it seems best to use the vocabulary for it that is most common in ordinary language. While, on the one hand, this may raise some misunderstandings which I shall attempt to eliminate as we go along, it does advantageously bring the language of the specialist closer to the language of the street. This can make the contributions of specialists more accessible and relevant to the general public as well as giving the specialist easier access to 'common wisdom' abroad in the culture that may be found in, for instance, novels rather than texts. The writer of stories is as much concerned with what makes people 'tick' as the psychologist is and here again there are areas where mutual learning is possible.

The story-teller is certainly concerned with the irony of life and its sometime undoing, sometimes tragic or comic consequences, and this is a domain where therapists would, broadly speaking, benefit from a wider acquaintance. Stories turn on relationships, either between persons or between persons and circumstance and they show how character emerges from and affects such relations.

Theory

This book offers theory about cultural appreciation and about psychotherapy. There is a circularity between the two areas that, in our age of specialised knowledge, is seldom exploited as much as it can usefully be. I believe that what follows below is quite practical in the sense that there is nothing so useful as a good theory. It is only partially a 'how to' book, however, and more precisely a 'how to think about what you are doing' book. Although it has its roots, as everything must, in particular sources, it aims to go well beyond them and so says something distinctive that is not wholly within any one existing school of psychological thought or branch of cultural and therapeutic activity.

Therapists have different ways available to them by which to frame their thoughts about what is happening to the client and what they are doing in their work. These alternatives constitute the different schools and theories of psychotherapy. They have differing implications for practice and intervention to some extent, though sometimes quite different theories can prescribe and provide a justification for the same intervention. A good theory should not only be able to explain the successes of people applying that theory, it should also be able to explain those of people approaching the matter in a different way. A humanist psychotherapist might explain the successes of analytic or behaviourist therapists in terms of the warmth of the relationship that they develop with their clients, for instance, or a behaviourist might discern differential patterns of reinforcement in the ways that the humanist and the analyst respectively respond to their clients. Each good theory can explain the other's effects in its own terms. I call them 'good' theories because this present work does not really attempt to refute any of the established (in the sense of 'currently widely used') theories. It tries rather to throw a new light upon the scene and to provide a new way of looking at human development, human problems and their solution that might be of interest to all.

In the realm of cultural criticism theory is even more diverse and though one can discern trends that one might call 'romantic', 'modern', 'post-modern', 'abstract', 'expressionist', 'construc-tivist', 'deconstructivist' and so on and on, there is really much less of an established categoric table of schools than there is in psychology, or, at least, the field is currently more fluid. Here contending ideas are, perhaps for that very reason, often espoused with even greater sharpness and the debates between different perspectives upon what is the "truth of poetry", to use Hamburger's term (Hamburger 1968) may involve even more invective than is now so common in psychotherapeutic circles, though, perhaps, even this comparison is invidious. Nonetheless, my perspective here is essentially inclusivist: we can learn from all without having to agree with all, and the theory advanced in this book does, I think, explain why some different approaches work when they do, though does so in terms that the practitioners of those approaches might not immediately recognise.

In neither arts nor psychology can we say that a theory is the truth, certainly not the only truth, though good theories do shed light upon some aspect of the truth of all, and in that respect my attitude is one that assumes that there is a truth, a reality, even if, for unavoidable reasons, it can never be discerned unequivocally or finally and, by implication, therefore, is outside the grasp of science if science is conceived as limited to what can be measured. Love is intrinsically ametric.

The theory in this book is similarly non-final. It cannot be a complete representation of what is there. It can only be final and complete in being itself; in being something that will be superceded. Even the key terms 'love', 'drive', and 'disappointment' each have a thousand shades of meaning and I am sure that by mischievous if not judicious selection among those shades the whole thing could, and by some parties almost certainly will, be made to sound ridiculous, but that too is part of human creativity, which I would count a guise of love. Such is irony.

A good theory explains phenomena in a simple and understandable way. It provides core concepts in such a way that one concept can explain many phenomena. It provides concepts that help us understand phenomena that are not intuitively obvious by means of concepts that do have immediate intuitive significance. A good theory, therefore, is not trivial. In psychology the non-obvious would include questions like 'Why do people sometimes hurt one another?' 'Why do they hurt themselves?' 'Why do they go on being frightened after the object that frightened them is no longer present?' 'Why do relationships that were once successful subsequently sometimes fail?' 'Why do some people work to the limit of their capacity while others seem to be incapable of doing so?' 'Why do we ask 'why?'?' and innumerable other such questions.

To address such questions one has to have a notion of 'how people tick'. We need theoretical concepts about the basic working of the human mind, psyche or soul, a terminology in which to think about such problems and some established pathways of thinking that enable us in many instances to think, 'Oh, that is a case of such and such' in a manner that leads us on to constructive thoughts about how to respond. This is equally true in our attempts to comprehend culture. So theory is more comprehensive than simply being a set of symptoms and remedies, or a schema for classifying phenomena, although it may imply or include such things. It is an attempt to provide principles that explain why such and such might be a remedy for or justifiable portrayal of a particular condition, or why such and such makes one cry while something else makes one rejoice and what crying and rejoicing may have in common, or have to do with beauty and satisfaction or ugliness and meanness, and so on, and in order to do so, the theory needs to provide a partial or total model of the person, and that means of the principles behind the way that people carry on.

All theories of psychotherapy do so. They all provide models of human functioning, core and derivative concepts, thought pathways useful to the practitioner, and examples of remedies. One might wonder why there is not just one theory. In the physical sciences it seems to be the case that theories are advanced and then tested, some are found wanting and discarded and others endure. In the field of psychology this does happen to some extent, but it is in the nature of psychology that it is much more difficult to prove a theory to be wrong than it is in the field of physics, say. In the arts it is even harder and often, even in principle, impossible.

Even in physics, however, disproof is not the only means of advance. Let us take a famous example from astronomy. A modern person looking at astronomy may say, naturally enough, that 'the idea that the sun goes round the earth has been disproved and the idea that the earth goes round the sun makes sense'. However, strictly speaking, if we think in terms of relativity, it is still true that the sun goes round the earth. There is no basis upon which one can establish a 'still point' in the universe that is not arbitrary. Ptolemy's theory is not exactly wrong and for everyday purposes we still use it when we say that 'the sun rises in the East'. We still think of the sun as going round the Earth, even though we 'know that it doesn't'. The reason that we use the Copernican model is that it provides a much simpler theory. If we think of the Earth as still, then the sun's course around it is extremely complicated whereas if we think of the sun as the still point then the Earth is seen to move in a harmoniously satisfying ellipse around it and complications disappear. By this example I hope to illustrate that in the matter of theory building we are not just looking for what is 'right', we are also looking for simplicity, elegance and usefulness. Several theories may be right, but one may provide a simpler and more straightforward solution to common problems than another. This, in science, is called Occam's Razor, or the principle of parsimony. If I have any claim that the theory of this book is superior to other available theories in the field, then it would be a claim of this kind. I wish to propose that an other centred approach often provides a simpler and more elegant solution to some of the common problems of life.

Other Centredness in Brief

This book attempts to develop the theory that I originally published under the title, The Necessary Condition is Love, in an article in the book *Beyond Carl Rogers* in 1993. Now, a decade and a half later, I still feel that this idea is central to my convictions and is a pivot around which my therapy work, my spirituality, my writing and cultural appreciation, and my relationships and life in community revolve. However, I have not until now attempted to develop it into a book length exposition.

Let me start with a brief summary of the central points. This book advances the following ideas

1. The drive to love is a core element in what it is to be a human being. We reach beyond ourselves. Life is meaningless without such. We find meaning not in ourselves but in what we devote ourselves to.

2. Humans also have a variety of self-preservative, self-nourishing, and otherwise self-serving drives, but these are secondary and, ultimately, derivative. If we group these drives together, we may speak of two basic drives, love and self-preservation.

3. The two drives set out above can be thought of as the strong and weak forces of human life, somewhat as the electro-magnetic force and gravity are the primary strong and weak forces that pervade our gross universe. Thus gravity is everywhere, but magnetism can override it (as you can see when a small magnet picks up a lump of iron against the pull of the gravity of the whole planet) and many scientists think that one day they will find a way to reduce one force to the other. In other words, selfishness is everywhere, but love prevails.

4. A telling symptom of the operation of these two drives is the manner in which a person (or group or culture) esteems. We are not here talking about self-esteem, which is something else, but about how people esteem objects that they experience as other (i.e. not self).

5. Adopting the principle that the drive to love is the primary drive has the effect of changing much of our psychological theorising and, in many cases, simplifying it, bringing it closer to the language of everyday, and making it more useful.

6. The theory has significant implications for understanding creativity and artistic activity and therefore for cultural appreciation in general. An examination of the field of creativity also throws further light upon what is required in psychological work.

7. This potentially offers the prospect of a degree of unification or harmonisation between the theory of literary and cultural criticism and psychology with gains for both, the theory revealing some of what is common between the role of the artist and that of the therapist.

8. The theory has concrete implications for the conduct of

psychotherapy and counselling suggesting, among other things, an object centred methodology.

This eight-point proposition gives us the core of what follows and may be used as a summary of the theory.

In some ways this theory puts into a slightly more formal frame perennial wisdom and common knowledge. You do not need to be doctor of psychology to know that selfishness is everywhere yet love conquers all, if sometimes tragically, yet there does seem to be an important job to be done in bringing such wisdom into the discourse of those professions that are concerned with the healing and improving of our souls or psyches on the one hand and our communities and culture on the other. At the same time, most people do seem to operate as though these basic truisms need not be so if only this or that nostrum of social or personal reform were applied, by dint of which we should all supposedly enter a time when an unassailable happiness will dawn. Yet it never does and never can and such idealism, also born ultimately of love, is bound to meet frustration and in the process often then gives rise to a variety of negative thought patterns, behaviours and wishes (motives). We end up both relishing disaster and surprised and alarmed by it.

There is, therefore, a double task: to come closer to obvious facts and also find a way of living with them that does not drive us into unwarranted idealism on the one hand nor despair on the other. This issue of balance runs through our theme. To do things 'for love' is different from doing them for an ulterior (self-centred) motive. Most things that people do involve some balance between the two factors. When most of what we do is no longer 'for love' we have become slaves, no matter how we may be rewarded. In modern Western societies many people have become cosseted slaves, living out an alienated, 'over-distanced' existence.

Let me begin, therefore, by saying a little about how I arrived at these ideas.

The Influence of Carl Rogers

The Theories of Carl Rogers

As mentioned above, in the 1970s and 80s I was much influenced by the work of Carl Ransom Rogers. I still am, though not uncritically. Rogers died in 1987. He was widely influential in the field of psychology and psychotherapy and also had some impact in education and peace studies. My own thinking developed in a mix of admiration, response and reaction to Rogers. It is about the current development of that thinking that I write here. I do not want to repeat the whole of Rogers' opus, since it is well documented in many other books. However, a brief recapitulation is in order to set this work in context.

Rogers passed the first twelve years of his career at the Rochester Child Guidance Centre in New York, of which he in due course became director. Harry Van Belle points out that "Rogers was an American who was born and raised in a cultural climate in which the dilemma of the freedom of the individual over against conformity to society was dominant." (Van Belle 1990, p.47). He was influenced by the philosophy of Dewey and then later by that of Otto Rank via the work of Jessie Taft. From this latter source he learnt much about therapeutic method. This mix of North American and European philosophies contributed to his creativity. In 1939 Rogers published *The Clinical Treatment of the Problem Child* and on the strength of this book he was offered, and accepted, a professorial post at Ohio State University. There, he became the first researcher to put recording machines, which were then a new invention, into the consulting rooms of psychotherapists and counsellors. He was interested to know the facts about therapy. A favourite expression of his was, "The facts are friendly" and this expressed much of his attitude to life, an attitude that to many Europeans would seem unduly optimistic. He wanted to get to the heart of the matter of what was going on between therapist and client that made a difference and led to therapeusis (healing, positive therapeutic change). He suspected that the theories of Freud and his followers that were then in fashion were overly complex, but he did not think that the behavioural approach of trying to reduce complex interactions to their component atoms, ignoring subjective consciousness, and looking for simple learning sequences was adequate. He was looking for a middle path that was non-reductionist, so as to respect the complexity of human beings as living organisms more than just sophisticated mechanisms, yet was not dependent upon esoteric concepts and circular reasoning that tended to generate a, to him, unnecessary degree of mystique and untestable speculation.

He felt that the key had to lie in the effect of basic human characteristics and he set about trying to define them in an experimentally operational way. Were there human traits that were sufficiently clearly recognisable to be measurable that could account for change brought about through relationships? Rogers thought so and in 1940 in an address at the University of Minnesota he talked about a 'newer therapy' consonant with the 'relationship therapy' described in his 1939 book. This was the beginning of the non-directive client-centred therapy that he was to spend many years refining. It is defined in an article in the Journal of Consulting Psychology in 1957 as having six elements:

1. that when client and therapist (or any other two persons) are in psychological contact, and
2. the client is in a state of incongruence, and
3. the therapist is congruent or integrated within the relationship, and
4. the therapist experiences unconditional positive regard for the client, and

5. the therapist has empathic understanding of the client's internal frame of reference, and

6. the communication to the client of the therapist's empathic understanding and unconditional positive regard is at least minimally achieved,

then positive personality change, which will involve an increase in congruence, in the client, will occur.

Rogers called these the necessary and sufficient conditions for constructive personality change. It was a bold theoretical claim in that it suggested that depths of understanding of personality theory were not necessary and that there was no need for the therapist to persuade the client to adopt a particular outlook or make a specific behavioural change. In fact, according to this theory, the therapist did not need to be more expert than the client in any respect other than in being more able to exhibit the necessary traits. This idea was a substantial challenge to the style of therapy being practised at the time and, although Rogers' ideas have since gained wide currency and are taught in many schools of counselling and psychotherapy around the world, the full force of what Rogers claimed remains a challenging doctrine. Much of the remainder of Rogers' professional career was devoted to refining the definitions required by this theory, researching their factuality, lecturing upon their application, writing about the theory and extending its application to other fields of human relations. In the last decade of his life he became predominantly interested in the application of these principles to the political sphere and the use of facilitators skilled in his methods in the reduction of inter-communal and inter-national tensions.

The Concerns of Roger's Followers

Throughout his career of writing and practice which had seen a number of highly significant innovations, there was a loosely knit community of people around the world who identified with and studied his ideas. The main concerns of this group were threefold:

1. How Rogers' work was to be protected and refined. His ideas seem simple but, like many things that are simple in concept, they are challenging to apply in pure form. There is, therefore, a constant danger of Rogers being misunderstood or watered down, and of people missing the full strength of what he was saying. This is made particularly true by the fact that Rogers' thesis is as much about what a therapist should not do as about what one should do. Many people accept Rogers' methods as part of a scheme of therapy, but it is an important part of Rogers' theory that the other elements of such a scheme be eschewed.

2. How Rogers' principles are to be understood. This question operates at two levels. The first is the question whether we do indeed really understand what he was saying, a question which leads to refinement of concepts, definitions and practical implications. The second is whether we have any understanding of how it works. Much of the drift of Rogers' theorising runs against the idea of mechanism so any questioning of "how it works" runs the implicit risk of destroying the theory that is under investigation. On the other hand trying to delve deeper through asking, "How is this happening" seems an obvious area in which to seek deeper understanding.

3. Whether Roger's approach is capable of further development and if so how. Precisely because Rogers' theory is so simple it has an air of finality that is hard to tamper with.[3] A more rambling or less coherent theory might offer a stronger invitation to innovation. Though Rogers himself clearly enthusiastically supported experimentation and innovation, there is still something about his theory that makes that difficult to do.

During his own lifetime, Rogers had developed his approach in two ways, though the second he tended to deny. The first way was to apply his theory to new domains. What started off as a theory for one-to-one psychotherapy was in due course applied in education, in groupwork, in marital studies, in community building, in organisation development and in peace studies. Clearly there is no particular obstacle to extending this list. On the other hand, development within the theory itself is a less tractable subject. Most people close to him felt that they observed a shift between what Rogers did and said in his early career in Chicago and his later career in California. The shift was indicated by the change of terminology as his approach started out as Client Centred Therapy (CCT) and then became the Person Centred Approach (PCA) and those in his circle would refer to his contributions correspondingly as Rogers I and Rogers II.[4] Now Rogers himself saw this as simply a change necessitated by the application of his ideas outside the domain of therapy, but most others, and I was one of them, saw a more substantial change in that in the therapy situation there is only one client, but there are two persons. The person centred approach developed in the context of the encounter group movement, and in encounter groups each person is self-expressive whereas in the therapy room the client is self-expressive while, for the greater part, the therapist is self-effacing. In research studies "The therapists were perceived by listeners as disappearing in deference to their clients" (Bozarth 1990, p.60). The shift from CCT toward PCA implied a greater focus upon self and self expression. This present work explores, inter alia, what happens if you move in the contrary direction, take the client centred (other centred) paradigm as key and go on to consider not only therapist's effacement before the client but the potential effacement of the client before a world of significant others.

Given this direction over time, from CCT toward PCA, which keyed well with the spirit of the time in which Rogers lived in which self-expression was becoming more and more a key value especially with younger people and was associated with ideas of democracy and escape from hierarchical social control, the earlier notion of the therapist's self-effacement tended to fade. It is clear enough that in client centred therapy, the therapist is asked to put the client's world in the centre of his attention. This is an altruistic activity that is not self-expressive for the therapist except in the removed sense that he is doing work that he has chosen to do. In the person centred approach there tends to be a stronger sense that each person should be self-expressive. This has led to the work of those who followed Rogers tending to develop in particular ways which I do not need to review here. My concern is simply to underline that the early Rogers had an important element of self-negation that appears not to have been generally experienced as onerous or oppressive by the therapist. This element of self-effacement is not alien to the theory that will be developed here.

It is possible, therefore, to see OCT and OCA as an outgrowth of CCT and the earlier Rogerian approach, taking it in the opposite direction to that later adopted by the PCA movement and, to a degree, Rogers himself.

Origin of the Theory that The Necessary Condition is Love

It was against this background that I presented a paper in 1991 at the Conference on Client-centred and Experiential Therapy in Stirling in Scotland called 'The Necessary Condition is Love'. This paper was subsequently published in the book *Beyond Carl Rogers* (Brazier 1993). The central idea of this paper has remained, in one way or another, at the core of my thinking and practice ever since, even though my subsequent interests have taken me into a variety of fields. I have written a number of books on psychology and spirituality since then. The present work is inspired by a sense that it is time to take stock of my present thinking on the thesis that the necessary condition is love. Let me therefore recap upon what this hypothesis suggests. I don't think that I can do better than to quote from the original paper:

"In person-centred therapies the therapist is invited to have an unconditional positive regard for the client. The therapist puts self aside in order to give full attention to the client. Providing accurate empathy is a thoroughly altruistic activity. Being a therapist, or indeed a helper of any description, involves 'a relationship in which at least one of the parties has the intent of promoting the growth, development, maturity, improved functioning, improved coping with life of the other' (Rogers 1958 in CRR p.108).

"The client's part in this endeavour is, by contrast, to focus upon self. The test of therapeutic effectiveness commonly assumed is whether or not the client's perception of and attitude toward self changes. The client focuses 'inwardly'. By doing so, the client makes contact with the felt sense at the edge of awareness. By following this 'edge' the client 'actualizes' the 'self'......

".... the first question I wish to raise is whether the therapist also is 'self-actualizing' in the course of therapy. Rogers hypothesised that the role of client is growth promoting, but, we may ask, is this also true for the role of therapist?.....

".... if the role of therapist is growth promoting, that is, if the process is therapeutic for the therapist as well as for the client, then it would appear that this reveals another set of 'sufficient conditions' different from the ones that [Rogers'] theory suggests are 'necessary'.

"After all, the client is probably not providing the therapist with accurate empathy nor unconditional positive regard, and in Rogers' theory the client is by definition, incongruent. So if the therapy process is growth promoting for the therapist then we may be saying that it is growth promoting to give primary attention to someone other than self, to put one's own concerns aside and to adopt a completely altruistic stance whether or not, in the process, one receives empathy, positive regard and congruence oneself......

"Intuitively, one feels that we have to assert that the role of therapist is itself growth promoting. Insofar as Rogers himself, in his own life, may have been said to have been 'self-actualizing' this was surely more by virtue of his practice as a therapist than by himself being a client." (Brazier 1993 pp. 73-74).

I went on to suggest that if one is, as a client, in receipt of the benign conditions described by Rogers, then there are many ways that one might respond, but simplistically one might either regress and receive the care directed toward one in a narcissistic fashion, or, one might internalize what is being directed toward one and oneself then start to adopt some of the behaviour being so precisely modelled before one. Now, insofar as clients did the latter, they would themselves start to fulfil our second set of conditions: they would themselves become more altruistic, or, at least, alteristic, either in their interactions with the therapist or in those that make up their life in their family and society. Given these two options for the client, it is also possible that those clients who respond in a purely narcissistic fashion might include those who make little progress in therapy whereas those who learn might include those who do better. This hypothesis strikes one intuitively as not unlikely and fits with clinical experience. Were it so, then we would in fact actually only have to concern ourselves with one set of conditions after all, the second one. This stands in contrast to the person centred view for whereas in that approach, "The client is now expected... to take the attitude which the therapist has toward him and to apply it toward his inner experiential growth... to become nondirective, empathic

[and] open toward his own dynamic experience [and] to trust his experience to such an extent that he begins to identify with it" (Van Belle 1990, p.51) in this approach it is anticipated that the successful client is that one who takes the attitude of the therapist and applies it to others.

"It is possible, therefore, that there is in fact only one set of conditions after all, the second set rather than the first. If this were the case, then the effectiveness of the first set would be proportional to their effectiveness in bringing the second set about and the failures of the first set would be accounted for by that proportion of clients who receive the therapist's warmth, acceptance and understanding but fail to learn to act in similar fashion themselves.

"Now, if it is actually the altruistic stance which is growth promoting rather than being in receipt of altruism, and if the value of being in receipt of it is not so much the gaining of its direct benefit but the opportunity to learn, or relearn, to adopt such a stance oneself, then our original analysis of the therapy situation takes on a different hue.

"We now see that the activity of being a therapist is intrinsically growth promoting while the activity of being a client is only growth promoting insofar as the client learns to adopt the altruistic stance. Therapy is more consistently good for therapists than it is for clients. Another important implication is that according to this new theory, unlike the original one, there is no fundamental difference between client and therapist. Both are trying to do the same thing, something which Rogers seems to have sensed intuitively but to have had difficulty formulating." (Brazier 1993, p.75).

Love Drive and the Actualising Tendency

Brian Thorne writes, "Rogers came to believe that there is only one single, basic human motive and to this he gave the name 'the actualizing tendency'." (Thorne 1992, p.26). The contention of this book is that it is at least as useful, as parsimoniously explanatory of human behaviour and sentiment, as elucidating of what happens in social relations, in cultural development and in the whole range of human development, creativity and pathology to assert that there is one single, basic human motive and to this we may appropriately give the name 'love'. It is out of the need to love and its vicissitudes that all other psychological phenomena emerge and develop. This is how being a therapist inherently tends to be fulfilling whereas being a client may or may not become so. It is the purpose of this book to argue for this perspective and to show how at least many such significant phenomena can be more usefully understood in this way. Please note that it is not really the aim of this book to refute rival theories in the sense of proving them wrong or dysfunctional, merely to say that understanding life in terms of love works just as well and often better and yields a simpler more straight-forward explanatory schema.

Thorne continues, "In common with the rest of the created order the human being, in Rogers' understanding, has an under-lying and inherent tendency both to maintain itself and to move toward the constructive accomplishment of its potential. Just as a tulip instinctively moves towards becoming as complete and perfect a tulip as possible, so the human being moves towards growth and fulfilment and the accomplishment of the highest possible level of 'human-beingness'" (Thorne 1992, p.26) Now here we have to try to be quite precise about what it is that we think is right about this and what could be improved upon as a theoretical formulation. The contention of esteem theory is that "fulfilment" is a function of the sense of satisfaction of the love drive. We feel fulfilled when we are able to love effectively and discontent when we cannot. The modes via which humans express their love and choose love objects are extremely diverse, but we all have an intuitive sense of the commonality of motive between the man who loves a woman, the artist who loves her work, the patriot who loves his country, the priest who loves her God and so on. In each case there is a love object beyond the self. The love object may be concrete or may be an abstraction, but it is something that calls the person beyond himself and that he or she calls toward and projects their energy toward in a variety of ways, nurturing, creative, protective, celebratory and so on.

Further, one does not love primarily in order to become as perfect a version of oneself as possible, even though that may in fact be the effect. The perfect human being is in some sense the perfect lover. The person who loves most perfectly is our ideal. However, a person does not love in order to be perfect. The tendency toward a kind of full self-realisation may be a fact, but the motive is something else: the motive is love. So we see immediately that we need to be careful to distinguish between motive and tendency. There may well be a tendency for character to develop through the vicissitudes of life, but one handles each situation with a motive particular to one's relation to that situation and the ideal and we here suggest the most basic form of that motive is love. So we are saying that love is the prime mover, and it may be fulfilled or not. Both theories suggest that a person does grow naturally toward fulfilment given the right conditions, but they differ at least slightly in their understanding of what fulfilment is and they differ more fundamentally in their formulation of what is going on, especially in respect to the fact that Rogers' theory posits a self-actualising self as primary whereas an other centred approach suggests that self-actualization when it occurs is secondary and not the primary concern. A person may self-actualize (in Rogers' sense) in the course of trying to live a life of love or may fail to do so. We can accept that there may be a broad tendency in the direction of actualisation, but not that that is the motive force.

Many thinkers recognise that a person is inherently incomplete. Love is then commonly interpreted as springing from the need of the self to become complete or of the individual to actualise herself. This may be a Ptolomaic solution. It is simpler to say that the self goes around love than that love goes around the self. If the self is primary, then there is no particular reason why it should be considered incomplete as it is doing what it does, and so it is difficult to explain why it would be valuable or satisfying to cherish another, whereas if love is primary, then love doing what love does, which is to esteem the other, explains everything quite easily and explains directly why the self has longings that are sometimes expressed as a sense of incompleteness.

Following the self-actualisation idea, Thorne says, "Just as the tulip is unlikely to flourish in poor soil and without proper care and watering, so too, the growth of the human being will be stunted if the conditions for the encouragement of the actualizing tendency are unfavourable." (Thorne 1992, p.26) In parallel distinction, esteem theory suggests, and it seems more obvious, that the path of true love does not run smooth and, in consequence, the person faces many challenges. In the attempt to love one runs into the paradoxes of this world. It is impossible to love one thing without destroying others. The ways that one attempts to implement one's love often fail. The love one offers is not always recognised or received. The object of one's love may respond badly or may be lost. Love has a hard time and so the person has to develop a range of strategies in order to go on loving somehow. Character is built out of our response to love's failures. To love one's country may result in building bigger weapons or walls and to protect one's loved ones may result in all manner of hardship and conflict. One reason that theory has often avoided the term love is surely the anxiety that its adoption might lead to an excessively optimistic view of human nature or the human situation. When one considers the travails of love that are so obvious and well known to literature, however, one sees that this anxiety is ill-founded.

Other centred theory is not saying that all this happens in the service of a more fully developed self. It is saying that what we might call 'self', but might better call character, develops out of the evolution of a range of strategies to attempt the unequal task of going on loving despite everything. In the course of life we pass through many dark passages. Our loved one's may be mortally threatened. Do we take up arms and go out to defend them, knowing that by doing so we shall, if successful, destroy other beings who are also fundamentally lovers and love objects for those that we do not know and that if we fail we shall bring grief and pain to those we love through their loss of us? Or do we not act and see our home overrun with equally terrible consequences? In the midst of mundane everyday existence we face innumerable small invidious choices about how to spend our time and deploy our limited resources. Does the young spouse go out and work long hours in order to provide for a family and in the process become unavailable to them, or stay home and see them suffer from paucity of resources that could be obtained by going forth? It is precisely these kinds of struggles that are the common stock of life that make character. They spring from the attempt to love in difficult circumstances more directly than from an attempt to actualise a 'self'. Without the love drive as a fundamental, they actually make little sense. If a person were simply concerned for self then none of these situations would be dilemmas, or would be much weaker dilemmas than they in fact are. In the idea of self-actualisation as motive, it becomes quite complicated to explain why a person would be self-sacrificing, but from an esteem theory point of view, it is quite obvious that self-sacrificing activity of some degree would be and is an everyday occurrence. Nor is self-sacrifice necessarily a hugely notable matter. In its smaller manifestations it is normality. Humans accommodate one another in small ways all the time.

Now it is possible in principle to reconcile esteem theory and Rogers' idea of the self-actualising tendency if we posit that self-actualisation is that condition in which one loves others. This stretches the concept, perhaps beyond breaking point, but perhaps not quite. The use of the terminology "self-"actualisation suggests that this is not an other-oriented state. However, Rogers himself does say, "I feel enriched when I can truly prize or care for or love another person and when I can let that feeling flow out to that person." (Rogers 1980, p.20). It is clear from the opening chapter of the book, *A Way of Being*, from which this quotation is drawn, as well as from experience of the kind of encounter groups that Rogers facilitated that one of the things that they bring about is an enhancement in the capacity of individuals to connect with their feelings of love for others and there can be no doubt that Rogers conceived his whole theory within an assumption of the vital importance of relationship. Rogers, due to his own preference, and the individualistic spirit of the times, tends to emphasise the receptive side of the encounter, the satisfaction people feel in being loved, but it is also quite clear that people are learning (or relearning) to love. It would be difficult and inappropriate to imagine that this capacity to love were not at least a significant part of what Rogers meant by being self-actualised, but it is doubtful if his theory would have met with acclaim in scientific circles in his time if he had said so. It was also strategic for him to use more technical sounding terms like 'unconditional positive regard'. The use of the term self-actualisation does, however, contain while disguising this (more) important aspect of the goal of psychological healing.

Ego, Libido and Esteem Theory

Let us turn for a minute to a comparison - a different approach to psychotherapy: the theory of Sigmund Freud. Freud's approach is generally dualistic. He asserts that there are two basic drives deriving from the ego and the libido, that is from the need for self-preservation and the need to reproduce. Freud's notion of libido is close to what we are here calling a love drive or need to esteem (not be esteemed). Ego needs derive from the reality principle. In other words, the ego is a result of the organism's encounter with the frustrations of existence. Strictly, therefore, the ego drive is derivative from the libido. Freud tends to give the ego drives a certain priority, nonetheless. He vacillates between the idea of a "primary and normal narcissism" (Freud 1991, p.66) and the idea that narcissism is "libido that has been withdrawn from the external world and has been directed to the ego" (*ibid*. p.67). Indeed the struggle to understand the real nature of narcissism was one that troubled Freud over many years and we owe a great deal to his reflections on the subject and to the work of some of his successors in that field. From an esteem theory perspective we could see the libido as equivalent to our strong force, the love drive, and ego needs as equivalent to our weak force, the reflexes that serve self-preservation that serve the love need, but which love may over-ride. This equivalence holds over a range of theorising.

In his later years Freud developed his idea of the ego drive into that of the death instinct, later to be referred to by others as 'thanatos'. At this stage of Freud's theorising we see the two instincts as of more of less equal valency. One could speak of the personality as a two wheeled chariot with eros and thanatos as the two wheels.

It is interesting to stop for a moment and consider how Freud arrived at the idea of thanatos. The ego drive was originally conceived as the urge toward self-preservation. However, it is apparent that we do die sooner or later. Initially, therefore, Freud assumed that there was something in us that wants immortality; a not incredible speculation. Later, however, he started to reason that, given that people do often make a good or acceptant death and do not always "rage against the dying of the light" (Dylan Thomas) perhaps it was not so much a case of continuing at all cost, but of dying at the right time. He therefore started to see the ego as struggling to ensure that one avoid premature death, or, to put it the other way about, that one die at the right time. To die in the right way at the right time would seem the logical conclusion of any kind of drive toward self-actualisation. Hence the ego instinct, in Freud, slowly transformed into thanatos, the death instinct.

Going back to the two wheeled chariot image, the early Freud did nonetheless see the ego as derivative, as a package of energy split off from the id under the necessities created by reality. The other centred approach tends to follow this line too. It is the need to love that is primary and if one is to love then one has to survive in order to do it. The wheels of the chariot are thus not ultimately equal, even though they might have to become so in the exigencies of real life. One derives from the other under the necessity created by unavoidable contingent circumstance.

Further, esteem theory would also go along with Freud in his assertion: "A strong egoism is a protection against falling ill, but in the last resort we must begin to love in order not to fall ill, and we are bound to fall ill if, in consequence of frustration, we are unable to love." (Freud 1991, p.78). However, Freud developed these lines of thinking almost exclusively in the direction of trying to understand psychopathology and one of the consequences of this was that he gradually came to see many things as pathological that we and others would see as healthy. How did this happen?

Broadly, Freud reasoned that psychopathology must be the result of the efforts that the patient makes to fulfil his or her instinctive drives in the world that presents them with reality constraints. This means that there can be clashes of three basic kinds: between the instincts, i.e. between ego and libido (as, 'shall I give up my career prospects in order to pursue the woman I love?'), between ego and reality (as, 'though imagining myself to be the most gloriously successful exponent of my profession I see my work does not in fact meet with mass approval'), or between libido and reality (as, 'I love her but she spurns my expressions of affection'). All of this is the material of which literature is made and so clearly speaks to the mass of the population. If our drives are conflicted or frustrated, then we usually have only a limited range of alternative strategies available. Some of these strategies constitute psychopathology. The person who develops hysterical paralysis and so cannot go into battle does satisfy an ego need in that he survives. This does not mean that the paralysis is not real - it may well be - but it is psychogenic. Similarly, the person who becomes ill thus making it difficult for his spouse to leave his side does avoid having to face what may happen if she goes out into the world and meets other men. Psychopathology thus has what is sometimes called 'secondary gain'. There is a pay-off. Freud realised that much psychopathology worked as if in this way. I say, "as if" because we are not talking about situations where the subject has the least idea that that is what they are doing. A third party can, perhaps, see the secondary gain in the situation, but the patient has not developed the illness with any consciousness that that may be what they are doing, and, if faced with such an idea will probably deny it. This is part of the story of how Freud developed the idea of the unconscious to such a high level of explanatory significance. He initially thought that cure could be effected by bringing the unconscious motivation to consciousness. He was right that sometimes a cure is accompanied by some aspects becoming conscious, but it is more likely that a 'cure' will actually come about by the person finding an even better method of meeting the instinctive need. This does not lead to heightened consciousness of the relevant factors but, if genuinely successful, to the whole matter being forgotten. *En passant*, let us note that this means that consciousness or awareness may serve a transient purpose in psychotherapy, but is certainly not its goal. This line of reasoning proved very fertile and helped Freud to develop a highly complex body of theorising and therapeutic practice and to say important things about a number of non-obvious phenomena (like why trauma-tised people go on reliving their trauma in imagination when this is evidently painful, and so on) that have in many cases still not been bettered. So why did all this lead him toward a negative view of a wide range of normal psychological phenomena as well?

As he developed the idea that psychopathology was due to the diverting of energy away from normal outlets he came up with a general theory of the economy of psychic energy. If libido and ego are conceived as having so much energy each, then the energy of libido could in theory go into performing the sexual act every time the impulse arose. However, in practice, this cannot happen so the energy has to go somewhere else. Some of the other places it might go were into the creation of psychopathology which was what Freud was most interested in. He thus talked of repression. On the other hand, especially in later life, he became interested also in other social and historical phenomena and suggested that culture and religion might also be a result of displaced libido and ego energies, especially the former. He wrote a number of studies of culturally iconic figures showing how their genius could be considered to have resulted from frustration of libidinous instinct. The most famous of these was his study of Leonardo da Vinci of whom he wrote: "the accident of his illegitimate birth and the excessive tenderness of his mother had the most decisive influence on the formation of his character and on his later fortune, since the sexual repression which set in after this phase of childhood caused him to sublimate his libido into the urge to know, and established his sexual inactivity for the whole of his later life." (Freud 1985, p.229).

There can be little doubt that Freud hoped that his work might shock people out of a kind of smugness or complacency that had caused them to act in ways that had been to the disadvantage of his career on a number of occasions. Showing that a cultural hero like Leonardo was what he was as a result of sexual frustration was a way of throwing down a gauntlet. More on this later. Freud's theory, however, can be reworked in a different light. After all, if we simply changed this statement to: 'Leonardo became what he became as a result of the frustrations caused by the obstacles that he encountered in his attempt to live a life of love,' then there might be a somewhat different response. Freud was only interested in pathology and so tended to see everything as pathology. Thus, "Since artistic talent and capacity are intimately connected with sublimation we must admit that the nature of the artistic function is also inaccessible to us along psychoanalytic lines" (*ibid.*). Despite this disclaimer Freud cast, and knew that he cast, an aspersion over it that suggested that things were not as nice as bourgeois society wished to think.

Sublimation

Redirection or Highest Fulfilment?

In the passage just quoted from Freud we find the term 'sublimation'. In many readings of Freud, sublimation tends to be taken as virtually a form of psychopathology for reasons touched on above. However, the basic meaning of the term is the deployment of something, in this case psychic energy, toward a goal more sublime than its original purpose or primitive form. Freud writes: "Observation of men's daily lives shows us that most people succeed in directing very considerable portions of their sexual instinctual forces to their professional activity. The sexual instinct is particularly well fitted to make contributions of this kind since it is endowed with a capacity for sublimation: that is, it has the power to replace its immediate aim by other aims which may be valued more highly and which are not sexual." (Freud 1985, p.167).

Now, if we remove ourselves slightly from Freud's concern with the primacy as he saw it of bodily functions (after all, he was a doctor) we can say instead that the love instinct is capable of diverse and extensive forms of sublimation since love can be expressed in many ways and the carrying out of a professional activity can readily be one of these. Indeed, we do not need to think of such expression as a distortion at all. We simply need to acknowledge that love has a variety of expressions some of which are more sublime than others. Sublimated activity may not be a weak substitute, but actually constitute a more satisfying fulfilment.

Sublimation in esteem theory terms, therefore, becomes a matter of finding a more rather than a less sublime method of finding fulfilment of the need to love. An artist provides a paradigmatic case of a person who takes material that may not be sublime in origin and makes it so or that may have been at a lower level of sublimity and raises it to a higher one. The artist who paints a portrait does not seek to do what a camera does. The artist is not merely a replicator. The artist attempts in one way or another to render the subject's image more sublime by bringing out an aspect that others had not, perhaps, heretofore acknowledged or noticed. Much of the theory and criticism (in the best sense) of art is concerned at least implicitly with the question of what constitutes sublimity and how it is to be, or how it has been rendered. Since the aim of art is to increase sublimity, not usually in a simplistic way, it is inherent in the artistic task that the artist address him or herself to subject matter and make use of materials that are not already intrinsically sublime. Art thus involves a kind of alchemy of transforming base material into gold. Whether the artist has been successful in doing so, often in an unprecedented manner, is the question before anyone who attempts to appreciate a work of art. In this context, we can see that an industrial wasteland might sometimes be a more attractive subject for an artist than a sunset or waterfall. We photograph sunsets in order to try to hang on to the sublimity that they already have, but an artist paints a wasteland and enables us to see it afresh.

Nonetheless, it is important to reiterate that for the other centred approach the problems that Freud found himself in, having to defend his theory from vociferous and indignant attack on grounds that his ideas approached obscenity, do not arise despite the fact that there are some strong parallels between the two lines of argument. This is due to the differing valuation placed upon sex and upon love. If we say that culture is due to a sublimation of sexual drive it sounds quite different from saying that culture arises as an expression of the need to love. This is because we all already recognise love as sublime. Sublimation of love simply means to raise love to its highest and find for it its most properly consummate object. It does not mean to detach its energy from its original purpose and redeploy it in some alien (to it) fashion, but to fulfil its original purpose in the highest manner. All theory is rhetoric in some degree. The choice that we make of language is consequential. An other centred approach suggests that it is natural and indeed basic to our nature to esteem the objects of our world and that this process of esteeming constitutes love and that such love can be raised to higher and higher, that is, more sublime, levels. This is a theory that unites the goals of psychotherapy, art, culture, and indeed history.

Defeat and the Fulness of Love

Esteem theory suggests that sublimation may have been the most important of the many ideas that Freud put forward and that it is therefore unfortunate that he never fully developed the idea and tended to present it as little more than a form of benign repression. Sublimation is the manner in which those who make the most of life do so: by bringing love to its most full development. Sublimation can mean to esteem that which is most worthy, most sublime, and to esteem that, the esteeming of which is itself conducive to the purest love. That a person pours

their love into the activities that build an art, a religion, a civili-
sation, or one of its component parts such as a science or
profession should in no way be regarded as pathological. Freud
suggested that all the high cultural constructions such as religion
and literature were diversions of primary life energy which he,
wanting a biological footing, labelled sexual. Most of what he
says is not wrong, but the suggestion that these things are
themselves somehow wrong or perverse is unnecessary. Other
centred thinkers will say that high culture is created by the application of love struggling to find a worthy outlet even after many
defeats since it is love that endlessly seeks to make heaven on
earth, impossibly to realise paradise here.

We may even suggest that this is what Freud himself did.
Freud was a talented man who, in the grip of his basic drive to
love, did what society wanted of him by establishing a family and
a career as a doctor (the most respected profession). His love then
encountered defeat in the form of anti-Semitic prejudice which
blocked his path in his chosen profession. This disappointment
and rebuff redoubled his energy and this had several consequences. The first was that he threw himself into the solution of
new problems, problems that his society faced, but which, with
very few exceptions, nobody was giving attention to. The second
was that he was angry. How are we to explain his anger in esteem
terms? The anger is the expression of his frustrated love and it is
that excess of energy that he pours into his work. Sometimes it
has an edge of 'I'll show them' resentment about it. He hopes that
his book on the 'fathoming of dreams' will shock. He aims to
shock because he wants the whole structure of complacent
smugness that he has run into to collapse. That wish may be
angry in form, but it is not difficult to also see its core of love. He
wants society to improve. All social reforms involve anger, but
are fundamentally driven by love. We do not need to see this
wish as a purely selfish thing. He has suffered as a member of a
persecuted minority. He wants such persecution to end. There is

nothing selfish at the core of such a wish even though it may emerge in personalised anger or gloating sometimes. I am, therefore, inclined to see the individual in terms of larger scale processes. Due to perennial frustration we are imperfect. Even a great saint feels some personal satisfaction when a reform that he introduced prevails and chagrin when it fails. This does not mean that the reform has to be seen as primarily an outflow of selfishness or egotism: there is a strong force and a weak force, the latter will always colour the former, but it is a mistake to then conclude that the former is nothing but the latter. From an other centred perspective one is, therefore, inclined to put sublimation centre stage and not regard it as an epiphenomenon of repression.

Philosophical Note

Before leaving Part One, which is primarily concerned with setting this theory in context, I wish to make a brief excursion for the benefit of the reader who is of a philosophical or theological turn of mind. It might be wondered from what has been said if this book is entering the lists in the debate over whether 'love' or whether 'the good' is to be considered highest. Basically, the answer is 'no'. Thus, Kierkegaard, for instance, asserts that purity of heart is to will one thing (Kierkegaard 1961), nominates 'the good' as that one thing and then analyses what gets in the way of such a will. Here, the 'will that wills the good' is taken to be love. There is thus no conflict. To consider 'the good' is to look at the matter from the philosophical or theological angle and to consider the drive, love, is to consider the psychological and cultural aspect of the same thing. My purpose in this book is psychological and cultural. At the same time, whether 'the good' is 'one thing' is something that one might take on faith, but which I do not think we can know. It is implicit in my thesis that we are imperfect and that it is not given to us to know 'the mind of God' even though we might revere it. The perspective offered here, therefore, is that love appertains to the lives of imperfect beings such as ourselves and an awareness of the fact of our imperfection is important to our being able to love in a satisfactory manner. Thus, 'sublimation', for instance, offers a useful direction, but what 'the sublime' may be in the ultimate case is something that we might conceive of but can never know just as love itself in its essential being is something that we never know except by its effects.

Part Two:

The Nature of Esteem

Unconditionality - For Nothing

In the light of the idea that the necessary condition is love, we can have a second look at the core conditions as presented by Rogers. What is going on for the therapist? She is viewing the client in certain particular ways and accompanying the client in an exploration of the client's world in certain similar ways. Let us single out as particularly important the fact that the therapist engages in an honest approach. We might say that the therapist is sincere, genuine or, as Rogers did, 'congruent' and this might give a gloss of professionalism or specialism to our language, but what is primarily meant is that the therapist engages in a scrupulously honest enquiry and is interested in helping the client to find the truth too. Note, the honesty or congruence extends not just to the therapist, but also to the goal. Therapy is an essay towards a more thoroughly honest communication than is common. This is one of its defining characteristics.

There is nothing contrived in our saying that this is one form of love. Rogers' would say, "The facts are friendly," that we have nothing to fear from finding out what is so. It is better to know. He had a deeply rooted confidence that truth was therapeutic. Helping a person edge toward the truth is an act of love and perceiving the truth may also be conducive to the growth of love. We might agree that this principle does sometimes need to be tempered, however. Not everybody is in a position to cope with the fullness of truth all at once. Nonetheless, broadly, Rogers is right that truth is therapeutic. This is true even when the truth is that some undesirable thing is the case. Every experienced therapist can think of situations where a client was released by arriving at clarity that the thing they most feared was in fact truly the case. The truth is better than the fear and uncertainty.

Such truthfulness can easily be compromised by purpose-fulness. As soon as therapist and client have a goal there is a temptation to manipulate appearances in order to make it seem that the goal is achieved or can be achieved. Somehow the thera-peutic activity has to remain clean of that kind of manipulation. Many 'pop psychology' works suffer from this error in gross ways. The practitioner's enthusiasm for a particular panacea over-rides even common sense.

This is what Iris Murdoch means when she says,

> "The Good has nothing to do with purpose. 'All is vanity' is the beginning and end of ethics. The only genuine way to be good is to be good 'for nothing' in the midst of a scene where every 'natural' thing, including one's own mind, is subject to chance, that is, to necessity." (Murdoch 1970, p.69)

and John Shlien is saying something very similar when he writes,

> "the most important objective in modern civilization is: *how to lead an honourable life*... Finding an answer to this question would not guarantee happiness, or serenity, or any other benefit such as social rewards. That is one of the strange features of this moral question. The only motive that makes it work perfectly is the strange idea: virtue is its own reward." (Shlien 2003, p.72)

Shlien's 'its own reward' and Murdoch's 'for nothing' are both trying to indicate the same truth as Rogers was aiming for with the word 'unconditional'. Now Rogers is surely right in saying that the ideal is an unconditional positive regard (or esteem) for the client, and one senses that we are intended to take this quality of unconditionality as a hallmark of the whole relationship.

This 'for nothing' is surely to be seen as the refutation of King

Lear's remark to his daughter Cordelia that "Nothing comes of nothing" (Lear Act I, sc. i). You will remember that in Shakespeare's play Lear decides to divide his kingdom and pass it over to his three daughters. He asks each in turn what they can say in order to demonstrate how much they each love him. The two elder sisters, Goneril and Regan each make flowery speeches - "I love you more than words can wield the matter; / Dearer than eyesight, space, and liberty; / Beyond what can be valu'd, rich and rare; / No less than life, with grace, health, beauty, honour; / As much as child e'er loved, or father found; / A love that makes breath poor and speech unable; / Beyond all manner of so much I love you." Thus speaks Goneril and Regan is equally lavish. However, when Lear comes to Cordelia, who is the daughter who really loves him most, she is unable to say anything. Lear disowns and disinherits her because she cannot come up with the kind of words that the two elder sisters could turn on so readily. We, the audience, know that he is being a fool and that the rest of the play will be concerned with the sufferings that he has to pass through as result of his folly in not seeing that the love of Cordelia is more valuable and authentic than the superficiality of the two elder sisters who later, when they have the power, abuse their father in all manner of ways. In an aside, Cordelia has remarked, "I am sure my love's/ More ponderous than my tongue." 'Ponderous' here means weighty or important, and we, the audience, agree. Goneril and Regan 'love' their father largely for what they can get from him whereas Cordelia loves him fully. Real love is not 'for something'. It is primary, or, we may say, 'for its own sake', or 'for nothing'.

This is our way of acknowledging its status as the strong force and primary spring in our lives. It is not secondary to some other purpose. There are simulacra of love and these are what we see on the stage portrayed by Goneril and Regan, but these are tertiary phenomena, conjured by self-serving motives and we all recognise them as false. Cordelia's 'nothing' is actually the mark of the completeness of her love and the tragedy turns on Lear's failure to recognise it as such. Murdoch's 'for nothing' is Cordelia's 'nothing'. They are the same.

Honesty and truth also have a 'for nothing' quality. They are also 'their own reward' and 'for the love of it'. To seek truth is to be open to finding what is so irrespective of what it might turn out to be. The contention here is that this is the duty of the therapist and that it is a form of love: that love and truth are two aspects of the same thing and both are unconditional. Love is the unconditional nature of the person and truth is the unconditional nature of the world and we are here looking at the point where they meet. The invitation of the therapist to the client, or, indeed, of the sage to the disciple, is, 'stop and look' - meaning, let us dare to see what is actually the case. The therapist is not looking for a 'happy ending' so much as an honest one. Even if the client is unwilling or unable to be honest, the therapist will not depart from honesty herself. It is not her duty to make the client see what the client is reluctant to see, but nor is it her duty to collude. In this dilemma lies one area of psychotherapeutic skill. The therapist in the ideal case is, as Rogers' says, unconditional in her positive regard for the client, even the client who does not want to look, will not see, or blatantly lies. The therapist is able to continue to be so because she understands that even these perverse symptoms in the client are the working out, albeit at a remove, of the love drive. The therapist's esteem for the client thus includes and extends to esteem for the client's story and for the characters that inhabit it.

The therapist will realise that the client always has reasons, even when they are not expressed. If love cannot flow easily toward truth then it is because love has in some way been blocked and this 'block' contains disappointment: a reservoir of pain. Lear disinherits Cordelia. He hurts the one who loves him most. As the plot unfolds his life becomes more and more distressing. He is extremely reluctant to see the truth. We might say that he is reluctant because in doing so he must face the harm he has done, the pain caused. His refusal to face reality leads him into madness. Though he had started out with the seemingly good motive of hearing how much his daughters loved him and bestowing upon each of them great benefit, his inability to discern true love when it appeared before him led to his downfall and to the time when "all's cheerless, dark and deadly", and, in due course, to the downfalls of all of the other major characters, though some, like Cordelia and the Fool die innocent and Lear dies of a broken heart for their loss.

The play increases our respect for true love and intensifies our concern for what happens when it is ignored or rebutted. In the final speech, the Duke of Albany says, "The weight of this sad time we must obey; / Speak what we feel, not what we ought to say./ The oldest hath borne most: we that are young / Shall never see so much nor live so long." (Lear, Act V, sc. iii). He is saying firstly that the tragedy that has unfolded is a natural development and must be borne as such; that there is a lesson to be learnt about speaking what we truly feel and not simply saying what is required (as Goneril and Regan had done); and that what we have seen is the extremely long life of Lear, which is long not in the chronological sense primarily, but in the sense that he has had to go a very long way through extreme pain and hardship in order to arrive at the truth about love. In one way or another we are each and all on a pathway toward discovering the truth about love, a truth that is unconditional and lodged at the core of our being-in-this-world, and along that long road there lie many obstacles, much pain and trouble, but we exacerbate that trouble hugely when we fail to recognise love as it is and are taken in by its simulacra.

So here we can see love and truth united, but if we were forced to separate them and ask what is primary, is it not, in fact, love? The reason that truth is sought is a loving reason. When love is not in play, truth may still be truth, but there is no motive for seeking it. Truth may be the primary quality of the world, but love is the primary quality of life. To return to our earlier analogy, which goes around which? The therapist serves truth as a high god, but does so because of love (positive regard). Love is higher for us, for we are not inert; we are not dust yet. There are, however, different kinds of priority. Love may be higher, but is it first? Can one love before finding truth? Surely one can, must and does. Which of us ever finds truth? We find fragments of it. We do not encounter it whole. If psychotherapy were foremostly the service of truth then it would ultimately be a case of the blind accompanying the blind. Similarly in the domain of spirituality. Can one help another before enlightenment? If not, then there is surely very little helping going on for the enlightened are rare. No, in human life, it is truth that orbits love not vice versa. We try to love and in the process try to be realistic, but even if this eludes us we still continue our various life strategies that are love driven even when unrealistic.

Those who help others do penetrate enlightenment. It is through their love that they encounter the truths that are of greatest importance: the lovability of the other, the ubiquity of frustration, the imperfection of all who strive for betterment, the esteem that can transform heaven into hell and hell into heaven. The nature of the ideal life as one filled with activity done 'for the love of it' and of the enslaved life where nothing is done so.

To Feel Alive

A close associate of Carl Rogers was John Shlien. Shlien was an original thinker as well as a remarkably proficient psychother-apist. In 2003 a collection of Shlien's ideas was published under the title *To Lead an Honorable Life* (Shlien 2003).

The opening chapter of that book is called "To Feel Alive: A thought on motivation". Shlien is pondering on the nature of schizophrenia and on sadism, two phenomena that perennially puzzle psychologists. In relation to sadism he reasons that the sadist is trying to get a reaction from the victim and, he suggests, doing so in order to himself *"feel alive"* and he speculates that this may, in fact, be a generalisable proposition: "The basic motive of behavior is to enable the behaver to feel alive" (p.10, original italics). Shlien thought that this motive must be learnt by the infant organism, though he thought such learning universal. It is a moot point whether a learning that necessarily occurs for all members of a species is to be regarded as a genetically in-built trait, and we need not linger over it. The basic point is that Shlien thinks that we all do things in order to feel that we are alive and that this requires us to extract evidence from others. The evidence that we are alive comes from others, especially from their regard for us. The person who harbours fundamental doubts about his or her own aliveness may, therefore, be driven to extreme measures in order to obtain validating evidence. Of course, the person who acts so may still not be convinced since he or she knows that the response was obtained by their own manipulation. It could still be the case that the sadist and his victim are both mechanisms lacking genuinely human being. This would be one reason why sadistic behaviour, once established, would be difficult to extinguish. The evidence that it yields, though intended to yield liberation from the condition, actually provides the opposite.

Shlien's observations bring out the fact that interaction with something beyond self is a necessary part of whatever the basic motivating forces of life may be. Theories that treat of individuals as self-contained units alone are bound to fall short in their attempt to describe what a human being is. Shlien goes on to develop this line of thinking a bit further in the second chapter where he seeks a criterion of psychological health. Here he speculates that "the health of the therapist is transmitted to the client" (Shlien 2003, p.15). The client does not just receive the conditions provided by the therapist, "The client recognises the health of the therapist, beyond his skill.... I am suggesting that

health is 'sensed' in the way warmth is felt... Perhaps appreciation of health is built into the organism as is appreciation of
'warmth'." (p.16). I feel that Shlien is here edging closer and
closer to an other centred approach.

He then suggests that "listening, carefully defined, should be
taken as a fully-fledged behavioral criterion of health", adding,
"If it represents health and security for the therapist, why should
it not be a measure of those qualities in the client?" (p.16) and
later says, "Self-understanding has long been considered a
measure of mental health. This surely does not mean, though,
that to be absorbed in listening to oneself is an ultimate ideal." (p.
17) and he asks "[if] the better one's health, the more fully one
can listen. Is this conclusion reversible in the sense that learning
to listen... may be productive of health? If so it would help to
explain why the practice of therapy is 'auto-therapeutic', as many
therapists find it. It would also suggest that group therapy
provides an especially advantageous opportunity to listen, and
thus to experience a state of health." (p.17). Shlien is looking for
a more active definition of mental health, one that tells us what a
healthy person can and does do. He singles out listening as a
touchstone. Now, this line of reasoning is quite similar to my
own[5].

It is not difficult to concur with Shlien's suggestion about
listening from an other centred perspective. Listening is a
common way of loving. To be handicapped in listening is to be
handicapped in loving and so if esteem theory is right then Shlien
is right in that respect, his idea being a subset of the basic other
centred proposition. He also points out how clients may become
healthy by learning one aspect of loving (listening) through being
exposed to the model provided by the therapist or, indeed, the
models provided by other members of a group. One learns or
relearns to love from peers as well as (or even more than) from
experts.

Esteem

To love is to esteem. Here I am using esteem in its positive rather than its neutral sense. The neutral sense simply means to establish an estimated value for something. The positive sense means to hold precious or dear, to respect, to think highly of or have a high regard for. To love something is to esteem that thing highly and to cherish it. Love always has an object. The object of love is an other. The subject of what is called self-love is dealt with elsewhere in this book and is another matter. To love, therefore, is to esteem an other, and this firstly means to regard the other as an other, that is, as one that stands in its own right and has value worthy of cherishment. In esteem, the other is an end in itself. Though it may be known to be one of a class it is not seen as merely an instance, but as unique. Its participation in this or that category is extra knowledge and does not contribute to the core of esteem as such.

The object of esteem is inherently satisfying. One engages with what is esteemed in the manner that we have just discussed as being 'for love' or 'for nothing'. What is esteemed is not merely a means to some other end. The esteemed is an end. One of the difficulties of psychotherapy is that the client is a means of livelihood for the therapist and this inevitably makes the client doubt the therapist's esteem. Similarly, true art is really priceless, but the sale of it for a consideration is also the artist's livelihood. The drives conflict. Self-preservation undermines esteem. Fullness of love requires that love be disentangled from self-serving. This also means that in the fullness of love the other is truly experienced as being an other and not as being an extension of self. Recognising that the other is other does not necessarily happen all at once and may be an ideal never reached. This, the true otherness of the other, is a vital part of this theory and one reason why I have chosen to call this the other centred approach.

Generally, then, in the real world, love is mixed with feelings of identity, attachment and clinging. Increased love implies detachment. At the same time, the positive valuation that esteem implies also creates a focus of attention. There are thus two tendencies, apparently opposite, one tending toward fixation upon and the other toward liberation of the object. It is, perhaps, the tension between these two aspects of the matter than generate love's charge of energy. They do not fundamentally contradict. When the love object is fully esteemed it does hold fascination yet is it regarded as wholly independent of self.

So the proposal is that a, perhaps the, basic drive in a human beings is the urge to love, and therefore to esteem, others inasmuch as they become significant to one. Or, between two persons who are in psychological contact, insofar as one at least is congruent in the relationship, that one will to that extent be driven to seek a way of esteeming the other and will find an inherent satisfaction in doing so and a commensurate disappointment in failing to do so.

Insofar as there is failure, the other may be perceived as unlovable. This will be frustrating for the perceiver. We would prefer our significant others to be lovable. What is lovable is, above all, one who exhibits love themselves. A person who loves is easier to love than a person who does not, though it is not impossible to love the latter. To love someone or something 'just as they are' is an ideal never fully reached, something that belongs to the domain of gods and buddhas rather than ordinary folk, a divine quality and, as such, itself a numinous object that also draws our love and devotion in religion. In this life we love with varying degrees of conditionality and investment.

Loving thus involves both a drive, here regarded as a primary element in human make-up, and a range of skills in behaviour and perception. There is skill involved in discerning what is lovable in another and there are also negative skills in the sense that it is possible to teach or condition a person to become blind to the lovable characteristics of others. One sees this last phenomenon operating on a large scale during warfare where combatants are taught to perceive the enemy in a manner that permits them to kill. There are also skills involved in perceiving the other's world (the other's others) and appreciating the esteem that makes that world coherent and meaningful. To love another living being is to love them *qua* lover because if one does not see in what sense the other is such one does not truly see him nor see what is loveable about him.

In the special case of psychotherapy, if we generalise, a person (the client) who has experienced disappointment in loving seeks assistance. The therapist is trained to discern and locate what is lovable about the client. Two things follow. The first is that the client learns some of this skill, the application of which in their own life situation changes other significant relationships for them in important ways. The second is that since the element in the client that is most inherently lovable is the client's ability to love, the detection and celebration of this part by the therapist is directly therapeutic. By recognising lovability in the other we generally facilitate a process whereby they become more loving.

While the above is simply said, it does not follow that it is simply done. Rogers, Freud and many other leaders in this field were quite correct in identifying the fact that simply informing the client of what is the case, however accurately, seldom does any good. Indeed it might even create an immunity in the client to hearing or recognising those truths. Rogers spelt out the needed attitudes in the therapist with some precision. The therapist models the loving attitude through unconditional positive regard and accurate empathy expressed congruently. It should be no surprise that the task of acting in such a loving way consistently toward a person whom others have already found to be inaccessible and intractable is inherently difficult.

Roger assumes that the 'self-actualising tendency' requires the provision of the 'core conditions' from outside rather in the way that a plant needs water. The plant then grows and the client similarly flourishes. Yet what grows is also love. Love begets love. The client becomes more outgoing and engaged in his world. He does not just come to love one thing; he loves many things. Further, the fact that the self-actualising tendency does need such outside supplies undermines any claim to its self-sufficiency. It is dependent upon significant others. To make relatedness to significant others the primary rather than necessary auxiliary element therefore simplifies things.

Expression of Esteem

To esteem something is to see it as an end in itself. Esteem does not necessarily require any expression. The things we truly esteem constitute the backdrop to our lives most of the time. They are our ultimate frame of reference. They do not need to be said. This implicit world of esteem is only revealed indirectly, for the most part, if at all.

When we do say "I like that," we might be making an expression that is entirely selfish, but it is more likely that there is at least a tinge of respect for the object. Even inasmuch as we are selfish in this transaction, it is still a ploy to derive something for the self from the other and thus implies a recognition that the other has something. This is true even when the object is inanimate or vegetable. "I like that building," implies that one recognises the building as something of worth, not in the sense of commercial value, but intrinsically. Even if one is in process of constructing a (defensive) self structure that includes an element 'I am the kind of person who likes buildings of that kind', one is still drawing upon a prior perception of value in the building. The worth in the other has priority over the worth that one hopes to accrue to oneself.

In our modern world we are used to attributing worth that is instrumental - 'How much could you get for it?' - but even that sort of worth implies that somewhere there is something that is valuable for itself. Even if one gets a price for something, one is going to use that money to obtain something and, notwithstanding post-modern theory, one feels that ultimately one is going to get to something that has intrinsic worth. To recognise intrinsic (rather than commercial, or instrumental) worth is esteem and esteem is the expression of love. However, it is a characteristic of modern life first pointed out by Georg Simmel[6] that if means are intermediate there can nevertheless be many of them, means leading to means leading to means... and as the chain becomes more and more elongated the person becomes more remote from the ultimate satisfaction of true esteem and increasingly lives in an over-distanced and depotentiated world.

Further, we are not free to express our love just as we like whenever. Indeed, it can and has been argued that the prime purpose of our complex social norms is to channel our emotional life into socially useful purposes. From the perspective of the individual this means that in any given situation there are only a limited number of ways of expressing one's meaning and intention and these may often do much less than full justice to the matter in hand. We may say that esteem is expressed through codes.

There is nothing esoteric about this principle, though the codes themselves may have esoteric or convoluted elements to them. We are all familiar with courtesy. The way we greet a person is socially structured. We say what we need to say by means of a code. How we finish a letter is a simple example. Nor is the abandonment of such codes necessarily more effective. Some things are simply difficult to say. Also, what a saying is taken as meaning depends upon the context and if the code is established then a great deal can be taken for granted whereas if the code is lacking then one has to start from scratch and this may be even more difficult. The father who never expresses any emotion due to his regard for social niceties who one day sheds a tear expresses to those in the know a much greater quantum of emotion than the person who knows no mores who weeps. We need, therefore, to think in terms of the expression of love and esteem through codes that both help and hinder such expression.

Of course, language itself is a code. There is a line of argument that is common these days that suggests that language is a barrier, but one cannot really claim that we would be better off without it; we would not. It is true that words are very rarely perfectly transparent, but that is life. Everything real is imperfect. Love is lived out in imperfection - in sin, if you like - not in perfection. Perfection is not life. I am persuaded by Louis Menand's analysis of this matter. Noting that it is asserted that poetry "calls for each word to perform at its full capacity" he goes on "We may choose to doubt this premise simply by noting that it is a rare occasion when one word will do, and by suggesting that in many cases this is not because one word says too little, but because it says too much. Our ordinary speech is marked by a cross-hatching of redundancies, retractions and contradictions partly because unobstructed words are too powerful; they carry too much significance into the sentence, and wordiness is a way of muting the force of individual words in the hope that the whole will be more compatible with the modesty of our intentions." (Menand p.57).

The Disappointment of Love

Love Meets with Obstacles

Whilst we have a drive to love and esteem, we are born into a world that makes it difficult for us. The world imposes pain and limitation. We experience pain in being born, in growing up in getting old, in getting sick, in dying, and we must do all of these things (Brazier 1997). Love's fulfilment brings us our greatest satisfactions, but along the way we suffer, and sometimes the fulfilment eludes us. So along with our drive to love we also have instinctive reactions to avoid pain and suffering. These have immediate survival value. Thus we continually encounter situations where there is a danger that our love drive, despite its ultimate supremacy, may be locally and temporarily over-powered. We might see these as times of (spiritual) danger.

To pull one's hand away from the fire is obviously conducive to longer life. One lives to love again. Psychological health is a matter of the different drives continuing to function each in its proper place. The fact that we do have self-protective reflexes need not lead us to think that they are our only instinctive equipment. It is commonly held that people are basically and primarily selfish, but whilst selfishness is ubiquitous, I do not think that it is what lies at the root of what it is to be human. To hypothesise, as we do here, that the drive to love and cherish is at least as strong and perhaps stronger, that it is the strong force to self-concern's weak force, gives us an important way of under-standing life. After all, people do tolerate even extremes of suffering for the sake of love of various kinds, love of spouse, love of country, love of God, and so on. Even in everyday life, people go through hardship in order to do a day's work, and work, directly (if done for the love if it) or indirectly (if done as a means) remains a form of love.

The self-protective instincts serve the love instinct by seeking to keep us alive and in operation so that we can love. However, in the existential world this gets complicated. There are many common real life circumstances in which conflict can arise between the two drives and these often present dilemmas some of which may be considered to be moral. These again are points of danger. When our plans (at some level, born of love) do not work out, when those close to us (whom we love) die or leave or change in unanticipated ways, when we find that we have no choice but to be separated from those we love or have to spend time with those whom we fear or dislike (because they threaten what we love), all these are times of danger because they are times when it is not at all clear immediately how to reconcile the different drives and at such points mistakes may be made that may be of dire consequence, as they are for King Lear. Much of the world's great literature revolves around the different ways in which people have tried to handle situations like this. Does the hero flee and survive to fight another day or stay and die and become a martyr icon to inspire others later? Whichever, it is unlikely that he or she will do so without some measure of 'personal' or even small minded thoughts and feelings about the matter. The fact that we regard such as small minded illustrates the fact that the 'weak force' idea is close to the instinctive judgement of the ordinary person.

The self-protective instincts interact with the drive to love. Although ultimately the former serves the latter, in the immediate situation it is not uncommon for the two to be in conflict. This means that self-protection may sometimes and in various ways make love more difficult. We find it very difficult to esteem what hurts us. We do not find it impossible and, in fact, most things that we love do hurt us at least from time to time, and, commonly, we go on loving, but the difficulty is real enough.

The contention of esteem theory, therefore, is that this frustration and disappointment provides the driving force for the development of character and personality. So long as the person goes on living, we may say that they do solve, in one way or another, the problems that life puts in their way. There is perennially conflict and there is always a solution, but some solutions are more functional than others. Sometimes the solution is dysfunctional. If I am having difficulty in a relationship, I may try harder to understand the other or simply decide no longer to see that person. A child may not have the latter option and may have to be more ingenious in finding ways to survive and go on attempting to love in a situation where they are abused. In every case, the person, if they survive, finds a 'solution' of some sort, has to live this solution, and has to make it part of themselves. It shapes character, for good or for ill.

When love is frustrated energy is raised, the stakes get higher and the situation becomes more dangerous. When I say dangerous here, I do not necessarily mean physically dangerous, though that might be the case, but rather what we might call spiritually dangerous. The danger is that the love drive may become overwhelmed or blocked. The contention here is that psychopathology is due to the blocking of the love drive.

Another way of expressing the same thing is to say that psychopathology is deferment. The love drive is so central to what we are that the organism goes on living (so long as it does) on the assumption that the love drive will triumph in the end, even after one's own death. Although love requires self-preservation up to a point, it also prescribes self-sacrifice. Both the weak self-protective drives and the various forms of psychopathology can, from this perspective, be all conceived to be instances of deferment of love's goal. When self-protection seems to have triumphed over love, we are seeing an instance of 'live to love another day'. When self-sacrifice occurs we are seeing an instance of faith in the ultimate triumph of love even beyond one's own interest or life. Positing love as primary makes all these common phenomena plain, whereas self psychology must contrive more complex explanations. It is perhaps not impossible, but it is difficult to say, from a self psychology point of view why one would sacrifice oneself or why self-sacrifice would be instinctively revered by observers.

Freud suggested that the ego was created by the reality principle. That the energy of the id, the unsocialised instinctive drives, came up against the realities of the world and created a kind of skin of defence mechanisms. I think that he was half-right. The alternative that esteem theory proposes is that the basic drive that is frustrated by life is the urge to love and rather than a skin of defence mechanisms the person tries to evolve a repertoire of strategies that will enable him or her to go on loving in spite of evidence that attempting to do so will prove difficult, painful or impossible. In the normal case this skin creates what we generally call character, a repertoire of strategies, knowledge, cultivated reactions and mores, ways of being, that enable a person to go on loving in one way or another. The other centred approach would not deny Freud's contention that one of the things that can happen in the development of this repertoire is that some of the means developed are dysfunctional and constitute psychopathology of one kind or another. The normal case, however, is that the person turns their frustration into a constructive way of life, learns and grows and becomes a worthwhile character. They become lovable. Their own love drive is still finding good enough outlets.

What is most lovable in a person is their own lovingness. Since we have already set out how the normal case is one in which the person's lovingness becomes twisted in various ways to meet the exigencies of what is normally a somewhat recalcitrant sequence of life situations, we can also understand that perceiving the love in someone is not always straightforward. It may require some patient study to understand in what way a particular trait owes its origin to a frustrated attempt to love and still in some non-obvious way therefore continues to embody that love. As humans listen to one another in a safe situation and attempt to understand one another in a tender way, such hidden love gradually becomes apparent. As it does so those people become more lovable to one another and each experiences the satisfaction, which we suggest is most basic, of being able to love one another.

The Neglected Child
Many years ago I worked as a social worker. One duty that one had was to protect children. Sometimes children are treated very badly by their parents. Sometimes their lives are in danger. In such circumstances the duty of the social worker is to receive the child into the care of the authorities and to then find a home where the child will be cared for. Perhaps we take a child who has been severely abused and we find some good foster parents who want only to love and care for the child. From a common sense

point of view one might think that in doing so one has done a good job and all will now be straightforward and the rescued child will heave a sigh of relief and be overjoyed to have found safety at last. Any experienced social worker can tell you, however, that it is very common for children in such circumstances to idealise the parent who has abused them and is now absent and to harbour fantasies that the parent will come back and rescue them from the foster parents.

The child will do his or her utmost to find a way to love the parent, no matter what the parent does to them. With the parent absent the flow of data that informs the child of how difficult this parent is to love ceases. Absence makes the heart grow fonder. Absence actually makes it easier for the child to believe that the parent is lovable and therefore to go on trying to love them. This may, of course, be very frustrating for the foster parents who, in turn, have a strong urge to love the child.

What of the abusive parent? Are they simply exercising a primary selfish drive in abusing the child? No, because this is the unusual case. The normal case is that the parent loves the child and this comes instinctively. We regard the abusing parent as disturbed or 'screwed up'. We understand that the abusing parent has arrived at a contorted way of seeing the world and we assume that this came about as a result of experiences that they have had that made living a loving life difficult. In all these respects, an other centred approach is congruent with common sense and does not need to advance a complexity of theorising to explain straightforward matters.

False Guilt

A widespread cause of human suffering is the sense of guilt. How is guilt related to love? We can immediately think of two common cases. In the simple case, a person feels guilty because they have done something that has gone against their love instinct. They may have, for instance, injured a love object. If one loves another and then hurts that other one feels appropriately guilty. Of course, we can now ask why might one do such a thing and, if we allow the basic theory that the love drive is primary, then it has to be the case that the hurtful action itself can be in some way traced back to that same drive. Perhaps there has been a conflict between rival love objects and, in order to assist one, one has hurt the other. Perhaps it is a result of misunderstanding the other and their needs. In any case, without becoming encyclopaedic, we can acknowledge that it is extremely common for us to find ourselves in the position of having, in some degree, inflicted pain, suffering or trouble upon the object of our love and there then results, one can say, appropriately, the feeling of guilt.

However, there is a second case that is also extremely common. This is slightly different from the first. Where in the first case one sees that one has clearly hurt the other, in this case one feels that one has failed them. Now it may indeed be that this is an accurate diagnosis. Perhaps through weakness of will, failure of understanding, one's own inadequacy to a presenting situation, or however, one has failed to come up to the mark. However, it is also common to have this feeling in situations where one has done one's true best and still encountered frustration. If I love somebody who is, for whatever reason, difficult to love, somebody who repulses my good offices and refuses my gifts, then how am I to continue to find this person lovable? Commonly enough the strategy adopted is to take the blame for the failure upon oneself. Love does not give up easily. This strategy is particularly commonly found among children[7] The position of the child is such that he or she has little choice of love object as far as the major significant human others is concerned and this is even more the case in the modern nuclear family than in the extended clans of yesteryear. If the child tries to love mother but mother is stricken with grief for her recently deceased parent, then it may well be that the child meeting repeated failure to elicit confirmatory response will start to feel that he is himself to blame. This is quite understandable if we take it that the prime need is to love. If the need is to love and love is failing then there has to be some effect at an affective level. When our love is not working we feel bad. If our primary need were self-preservation we would not feel so, unless and until the breakdown of the relationship started to impinge upon us in some more tangible way such as mother ceasing to cook dinner. However, we are all aware that the kinds of feelings we are talking about can be elicited simply by the slightest tone of a glance. We readily feel considerable inward pain in the form of guilt feelings when we construe the situation to be one in which our effort to love is meeting with failure. A child who has learnt this coping strategy of taking the guilt upon herself may be hindered throughout life.

Obstacles Through Life

Much psychological theory would broadly go along with the idea that trauma or enduring the pain and frustration of cruelty in infancy are pathogenic. However, an other centred approach does not lead to a special privileging of childhood except in as much as early habits often endure. The love drive is hypothesised to be working throughout life and it continues to meet difficulties. The nature of the obstacles may change, but adults are also capable of being scarred. Sometimes such scars come from the difficulties inherent in our existential situation, as when somebody dies. Sometimes they come from the mistakes and misjudgements that we make. Earlier we looked at the play King Lear which describes how an elderly man makes a mistake about love with dire consequences for all concerned. Anybody who doubts that the vicissitudes of love affect adult life directly need only consider his or her own romantic history where few will find a story of complete plain sailing, and if they do, then they can talk to a few friends.

There is a common idea that one of the reasons for love's

disappointment is the inherent difference between men and women. The woman being the bearer of children has a greater interest, perhaps, in stability than the man. Society allots different roles for men and women, less different than in former ages, but still different. As Lilian Rubin says, "There's no denying that things have changed. Many more men than ever before are now genuinely involved in family life, just as many more women are committed to work in ways that are new. And there's no denying either that the conflicts they suffer over how their time is divided, the decisions they make when they must choose, the inner experience about what defines them and what places them in the world are still very much related to their gender. Generally, men still are best at the cognitive, rational mode that work requires, so it is where they turn for validation. Usually women still are more comfortable in the emotional and experiential mode that interpersonal connections require, so that is where they look for fulfilment. For men, therefore, it's still work that gets their first allegiance, if not in word, then in deed; for women, it's still love. (Rubin 1983, p.28)

This may be the case. However, in terms of our theory, 'love' and 'work' in Rubin's sense are both forms of love. The conflicts and difficulties are a result of the problems that we have bringing love to fullness. If two people love one another, then the two want to be together, at least some of the time and the modern conventions of equality may actually make that more difficult when, for instance, both partners in a marriage have careers, each of which may make powerful demands. On the one hand, the more different men and women are in their ways of expressing love, the more misunderstanding there may be between them. On the other hand, the more similar they are the more difficult it may be to resolve the kind of real life issues that arise when her career takes her to California and his takes him to France. The bottom line is that there is no system that has no bugs. Life is like that. Love meets obstacles and they do not necessarily have simple solutions.

Then there are the problems that arise with choice and commitment. While the ideal of loving everybody and everything with full and equal intensity might be an ideal of sainthood, in practice, loving one object can and does prejudice our love for other objects. We choose. As Jacob Moreno (Moreno, 1934) perceived, these choices are immensely important. They determine the course of lives and their survival. Depending upon where we invest our love, so shall our life be. Commitment is an unavoidable aspect of life. Many 'modern' people find this extremely difficult. We want to have our cake and eat it. We do not understand that going in one direction means that we are not going in the other direction at the same time. Closing a door on something is felt to be not quite nice and an air of vague wrongness hangs over it. This, however, is a false morality that tries to keep everything on an equal footing. If we try to keep the option we rejected on an equal footing with the one we chose then we did not really choose and we condemn ourselves and those who depend upon us to limbo.

Choice brings values of loyalty and duty into play. These values suggest that morality is situational. The idea of situational morality is quite different from the ideas of codified morality on the one hand or relativistic morality on the other. I do not propose to give a full exposition on morality here, but simply to note the broad outline of the implication. Love demands certain types of fidelity. Loyalty to one love object can bring you into conflict with other objects. All this was once regarded as truism and was the basis of society. While it is still the real basis of society, it is nowadays less socially acceptable to talk about it. There has come to be a great emphasis upon equality and individualism that undermines special affection. However, nobody can be an individual without special affection. That this unavoidably entails conflict is an inconvenient reality that we must appreciate if we are to understand how it is that loving people can find themselves at war with other loving people or that through love a person may do great damage.

Rogerian Ambivalence Concerning Education

Let us return to the ideas of Carl Rogers. It is an interesting fact that Rogers was very doubtful or ambivalent about the effectiveness of education. His basic belief in the self-actualisation of individuals made it difficult for him to conceptualise or enact a teaching role wherein there was any degree of transference of skill or ability from teacher to client. He believed that all that was worth having would come from within the student. Thus,

"I found my way into being human in class by somewhat of a back-door entrance. As a psychological counselor, dealing with students and others in personal distress, I had found that talking to them, giving advice, explaining the facts, telling them what their behavior meant, did not help. But little by little, I learnt that if I trusted them more as essentially competent human beings, if I was truly myself with them, if I tried to understand them as they felt and perceived themselves from the inside, then a constructive process was initiated. They began to develop clear and deeper self-insights, they began to see what they might do to resolve their distress, and they began to take the actions that made them more independent and that solved some of their problems.

"But this learning, important to me, made me question my role as teacher. How could I trust my clients in counseling to move in constructive directions, when I was not nearly so trusting of my students? Thus I began a groping uncertain change in my approach to my classes.

"To my surprise, I found that my classrooms became more exciting places of learning as I ceased to be a *teacher*..... Though at the time I had never thought of phrasing it this way, I changed at that point from being a *teacher* an *evaluator*, to

being a *facilitator of learning* - a very different occupation."
(Rogers 1983, pp.25-26)

Nonetheless, Rogers continued to write books that were widely
read, that contained much information and, in effect, advice, a
strong philosophy presented in a tightly argued form. While
Rogers' confidence in his students is admirable and the effects
were good, there remains something inconsistent in saying that
one should not advise face to face but it is alright to do it via a
book. Generations of therapists have learnt from Rogers how to
counsel, how to make empathic response to their client, how to
evaluate their counselling practice, and how to do research in
which evaluation is a crucial element. They have done so in
substantial measure by emulating Rogers or those who have
themselves emulated him. How are these two aspects of Rogers'
way to be reconciled with one another, or, what can we learn
from their incommensurability? Surely something about Rogers'
devotion to the ideal of individualism and thus a resistance to
the notion that all does not 'come from within' even when his
own theory requires it.

The term 'individualism' was coined by Tocqueville who
made a crucially important study of American democracy in its
formative period and, while full of admiration for this social
experiment, was also alarmed by the psychological consequences
of trying to make freedom into a positive virtue and principle of
social organisation. Freedom is always freedom from something
(Midgley 2001, pp.13-15) and the more that one cuts away, the
more vulnerable one becomes. However, under the sway of this
democratic ethos people "acquire the habit of always considering themselves as standing alone, and they are apt to imagine
that their whole destiny is in their own hands... and threaten in
the end to confine him entirely within the solitude of his own
heart." (Tocqueville 1835/1945, Pt.2, 2, ch.35). It is this focus upon
individualism that has made it difficult for Rogers to cope with

the idea of education as a process in which one person receives something from another, even though his whole opus rests upon the need for one person to provide the other with the core conditions that he specifies and that I maintain the client then learns, just as Rogers' own students learnt them from him.

Rogers' misgivings about the authoritarian classroom are quite understandable and I share them. Experimental and experiential methods in education can be wonderfully creative and exciting and I applaud them and use them. I do not agree, however, that it is universally the case that "the outcomes of teaching are either unimportant or hurtful." (Rogers 1961, p.276).

The dominance of education by predetermined syllabuses, examination rituals, grading and performance indicators has been dispiriting and created generations of young people who learn how to jump through hoops, become cynical, study as a chore, and are more concerned about credentials than knowledge. This is much to be lamented. They have been taught to perceive learning as instrumental when true learning is for the love of the subject.

Yet, learning is something that does occur between human beings. I hope that you, the reader, will get something from reading this book, as, no doubt, did Rogers about his own books. I hope that if I spent time with you that I might learn something from you. It is no infringement of my rights for you to share your enthusiasm about a subject with me nor is it a betrayal of my true being for me to learn knowledge or a skill from you. These are part of the normal transaction of life. They serve our love needs. Some of our learning is instrumental. We learn how to do something in order to achieve something else. The 'something else' always in the last analysis comes down to love of some kind. When we see the advert in which the hero performs a series of superhuman feats in order to bring the lady a box of her favourite chocolates, 'all because the lady loves Milk Tray', the advert is successful because it chimes with something that we all instinctively recognise as being close to the core of our being. We will do all manner of things for love and those things include learning.

Education thus has a double relationship to the love drive: indirect and direct. Some things we learn instrumentally in order to have the means to love and some things we learn about because we love them. We naturally learn about our love object. As we esteem it we study it. What we learn may not necessarily fit a plan conceived in advance by an authority, and it is that authoritarian aspect of education that Rogers was most centrally concerned about. It would be a mistake, however, to go to the extreme.

The fact is that everything does not come from within. Very little other than basic bodily and mental capacities and the love drive itself does come from within. The primary drive, however, impels us into the arms of a world where there is much to learn. One only has to watch a young infant to see this. Everyday new learning is gong on. Rogers was impressed by this self-directed learning and wanted it to be the template for all learning. Fundamentally it is. However, we do not need to be extremist or overly simplistic about this. People learn because they love. They learn in as many ways as they love. Learning becomes a way of loving. It is a way of engaging closely and intimately with the world. The healthy person goes on learning throughout life and loves to learn. In all that I am in accord with Rogers. Learning, however, takes many forms and when we see it as an extension of loving then I think it is easier for us to appreciate this diversity. It will also bring us into harmony with the person in the street who naturally recognises that there is something superior in the action of a person who 'learns for the love of it' over one who 'learns because he has to'. Nor let us forget that the Greek *skole*, whence 'school' meant 'leisure' which, in context, meant doing things for the love of them (Pieper 1965, p.21).

Ideas of Self-esteem, Self-love and Self-regard

While we are looking at the distortions that come from adopting an overly individualistic view, let us briefly consider the widespread occurrence of solipsism and narcissism in modern life. It is commonly regarded as 'rational' to love oneself, or to describe a behaviour as 'rational' if it can be shown to serve the self in some way. It will be said that it is rational to help your friends because at a later date you may need them to help you. In other words, when one has found a line of reasoning that suggests that a behaviour is finally self-serving then one is permitted to call that behaviour 'rational'. Similarly, when an argument that is essentially circular reaches the point where it involves a personal benefit one is permitted to stop and say that one has found the reason. This is, however, essentially arbitrary.

All rationality rests upon axioms. The axiom in this case is that self-service is fundamental to human nature. It is this axiom that this book questions. Certainly there are elements of self-preservative and defensive reaction in a person, but the contention here is that they are a weak force in the human make-up while love is the strong force. If we were to say that it is rational to help one's friends because of love for them, it is a much shorter line of reasoning than that which tries to make the act self-serving. People do things because they love something and self is a secondary construction built out of what they learn in the attempt to meet their primary objective which is to actively love what they love.

According to the theory of Maslow (1954), people seek to actualise themselves only after they have met a variety of more basic needs like food and shelter. Maslow's theory is widely accepted though it clearly fails to explain commonly acknowledged behaviour. We know well that people will go without food and shelter if that is what it takes to fulfil their love, be it love of country, love of profession, love of family, or whatever. The self-preservation drives are a pervasive weak force in our lives, but the love drive is a strong dominating force. It is not the case that weak force needs must be fulfilled before strong force ones come into play. It is quite rational for a person to go without food in their attempt to rescue their relatives from a dangerous situation. We can see the weak force as logically connected with the strong force in a sub-ordinate way. One needs to eat in order to have the strength to rescue them. When eating serves loving we eat, but when the two point in opposite direction it is the love drive that prevails. Adopting this philosophy *changes what we consider to be rational* and the kinds of arguments that we advance to explain behaviour.

Similarly, it is commonly thought nowadays that one must love oneself before love of others is possible. However, firstly, there is no evidence for this as people are perfectly capable of loving others straight off. Secondly, the implication still seems to be that the purpose of self-love is to prepare one for the real thing which is to love others. If all one did was love oneself one's life would be rather pathetic. Thirdly, there are many double meanings in this kind of advice. What is called self-love may not really be self-love and there may be no need to call it so unless one is already committed to an ego-centric philosophy: self-love may be sensible when it is a sophisticated label for a form of loving others and, remembering what we have said about parsimony of explanation, describing it as self-loving behaviour is unnecessarily convoluted. Thus, a person might say that he is loving himself at those times when he is doing what he loves most which is, say, being with his friends and family, but this is actually a behaviour of loving others. In the other case, a person might say that she is loving herself when eating chocolate. Now even this is a rudimentary form of loving something other than self, of course, but, leaving that aside, self-indulgence is really of no immediate benefit except inasmuch as it does serve the weak force in our life. If we become thus refreshed and so enabled to continue with what matters to us, all well and good. While writing this book, I snack. It keeps me going. If, however, all we do is indulge more and more, then life becomes more and more meaningless. The germ of truth in the idea that one must love oneself before one can love others lies in the fact that the weak force requirements are ubiquitous and perennial. We do have to do at least a minimal amount of self-maintenance in order to stay alive and fit and replenished so as to be able to do the things that really matter that usually turn out to be some form of loving. So the idea that one must love oneself first is really an adage that it is only possible to continue to love others if one continues to receive sufficient supplies in order to do so.

The danger of the self-love hypothesis is that it tends to make us think that self-love is primary, which is not the case. If we were not going to love anything else then there would be neither need nor point in looking after oneself. Self-neglect may often be well understood in this way. If a person is neglecting to eat, wash, dress properly, and so on, it may be that that is a person who has lost any hope of being able to love. The frustration of their basic need to love leads to a deterioration in self-care. If such a person were to fall in love with another we would see a rapid improvement in their condition. It is more true that if you love another you will take care of yourself than that you must take care of yourself before you can love another.

Another aspect of this is that it is extremely doubtful if one can really love one's 'self' as it is. This is partly because one only perceives oneself in reflection. Some degree of distancing has to occur. This is basic phenomenology. The ego as subject, as Husserl would have said, is transcendental and not part of the empirical world. One can only love something that one calls 'oneself' after one has objectivised it in some way. A corollary is that it is probably impossible to 'forgive oneself' while one continues to believe that one has not changed. While I still think that that person that did that bad thing is me, I cannot really forgive him. It is only when I start to see that sinner as a 'me' that

I once was, but am no longer that I am in a position to forgive.

As a rule of thumb, all the qualities that are prefixed with 'self-' that one commonly reads about as virtues are more truly virtues when the 'self' element is removed. Esteem is more important than self-esteem, consciousness is more valuable than self-consciousness (which is a handicap), love is more valuable than self-love, confidence is a perfectly adequate term for what is commonly called self-confidence, and so on.

Related to all this is the philosophy that others are not really other. It may be said that we all 'inter-exist', that others are not really separate, that we 'co-arise', or that we are 'inter-dependent' with all things. This set of ideas also has a wide currency, a smack of spirituality, and seems superficially to chime with ecological principles. However, it is not a sound philosophy (cf. Brazier 2001, p.100 *et seq.*). As a matter of observation, I am not you. Nor am I the sun. Nor does the sun need me. I am dependent upon the sun and the light and heat it provides, but it can do perfectly well without me. It is a one-way dependency relation. We do not inter-exist nor do we inter-depend. I depend on it. The inter-existence idea thus reveals itself to be another variety of the modernist attempt to have one's cake and eat it. We do not like having to face the fact that we are often dependent and frequently powerless. Life is constructed so that we will go on trying to love even in this difficult situation. We shall do so better by recognising the situation for what it is than by trying to pretend that it is more benign than is actually the fact. In any case, the appearance of benignity is false, since if it really were the case that all depended on all, then the evil would be as necessary as the good, all real progress would be impossible and love would correspondingly become meaningless.

Part Three:

Art, Culture and Spirit

Esteem Theory and Cultural Appreciation

The Happy Artist and The Troubled Artist

If the primary need or drive is to experience the world in an esteemed way then it could be that art is one strategy aimed at satisfying this need. An other centred approach helps us to understand why artists are often troubled people. This fact is inconvenient to many psychological and spiritual theories and therefore in need of explanation. Becoming better adjusted or spiritually advanced sometimes renders one less rather than more creative. Many renowned artists had miserable or conflicted lives. If they had had successful psychotherapy one can have no confidence that this would have improved their work and one must have at least a suspicion that in many cases it might have diminished their creativity and deprived the world of masterpieces. It is unfortunately the case that insight can kill creativity.

According to esteem theory, the primary and perennial frustration in our lives is brought about by love's failures, occurring day in day out in small scale ways and from time to time in more major ones, sometimes creating tragedy. The person wishes to esteem their world and is frustrated in the attempt. I, therefore, suggest that at least some art is an attempt to re-esteem an un-co-operative world.

We can thus imagine two different scenarios. To put it over-simply, in one case a person becomes an artist in order to express their love and esteem. This is the scenario of the happy artist. In another case, the artist is somebody who has more than normal difficulty in esteeming their world and art has become their attempt to solve this problem. This is the tortured artist.

Much modern art can be elucidated in this way. Often such art depicts objects that are not conventionally regarded as beautiful or easy to esteem. If an artist makes a pile of bricks into a work of art, many members of the public may wonder in what sense it can be called art. The undiscerning assumes the happy artist approach as norm, where art serves the function of celebrating the naturally beautiful, the naturally esteemed. However, the happy artist, while she or he contributes to cementing collective celebration of beauty, may, in practice, make less of a contribution to human well-being than the artist who brings something that is conventionally regarded as ugly or mundane into the domain of art and sublimity. What the latter does is less trivial. Indeed, by doing so, they are doing something that is not dissimilar to what a therapist does. The artist who can make a heap of bricks into an artwork and find in it what is esteemable is doing something parallel to the therapist who discerns what is lovable in an unpromising client.

T.S.Eliot

When T.S.Eliot wrote The Waste Land (see. Eliot 2005) in 1921-22, one could say that what he did was to take the unpromising condition of the world around him and make of it a work with a distinctive form of beauty, a work that is commonly regarded as one of the most influential poems of the twentieth century. The work was written in the aftermath of the First World War. People in general were struggling to find what was estimable in a world that could create slaughter on such a scale. Often in such circumstances it falls to 'border people' to provide something therapeutic. The shaman lives on the edge of the tribe. Eliot, like his friend Ezra Pound, who was also of great importance in the same era, was an American living in England who spent his whole life in some respects an exile. He was a disappointment to his parents. Eliot's father died in 1919. "He had died without seeing any evidence of his son's capacity except for a few strange poems" (Ackroyd 1984, p.91). Eliot was married to an English woman who was in recurrent bad health, had serious 'nervous' problems and was later to die in a psychiatric hospital where she was committed as a long-term patient. This marriage was a cause of great conflict and pain to Eliot, cultural exile and troubled man in a troubled world, one generation of disappointment following another. Yet it was he who more than anybody was to create a new aesthetic sensibility that would remain a foundation stone of taste for the remainder of the twentieth century and beyond.

Saigyo

The story of Eliot warrants comparison with that of the poet Saigyo (Watson 1991) whose work in twelfth century Japan changed the conventions of poetry from that time on. Saigyo did not confine himself to historical, religious and courtly themes nor to cherry blossom, moons and palaces. He wrote poems about loneliness using motifs of marshland, poor people's huts, mountain villages in deep snow and other tropes that until that time were generally not considered proper for poetry. He too lived in a period of post war disruption and uncertainty in which his own family suffered and it is widely believed that he lived in flight from a troubled love life. So again we have a troubled individual living in troubled times who uses unpromising material to construct a new artistic idiom that then changes his culture in an irreversible way and helps to rescue his time from meaninglessness.

Examples could be found in other art forms - visual arts, music, theatre and so on. The point is that the arts may perform a therapeutic role for society in the sense that they enable a constructive change, making it possible for that culture to esteem things that were not esteemed before and to do so by establishing new modes of esteem. In fact innovation in art could be defined as the creation of new modes of, or avenues toward, esteem. This innovative work is often performed by artists who themselves have a need to find new modes of esteem in order to solve their own life problems and the work that they do in their attempt to do so is regarded as great art when it chimes with the wider social need. The artist in question may still individually have a painful life.

Sincerity in Art

In contemporary art criticism across a range of arts there is frequent concern with the 'sincerity' or 'authenticity' of the artist and his or her works (Trilling 1972). This concern primarily springs from a 'self psychology' bias in art appreciation, yet from the perspective of our theory we may ask whether the concern with the artist's sincerity and authenticity is a concern about whether he is lovable or if it is a concern about what he loves and makes lovable. All the world loves a lover. We have already suggested that art is a mix of expressing love for the object and rendering lovable things that might not at first appear so. By accomplishing such the artist demonstrates her ability to love and so makes herself lovable. The art provides a bridge to the artist's inner world. It also commonly offers new ways for love to function. Sometimes art is 'difficult'. The bridge is difficult to cross. The art object holds out the tantalising prospect that there is something here that can be loved and there is somebody (the artist) who has managed to love it in some way, but the receiver of the art may still find it difficult to enter into that particular love. Art often hovers near to a limit. Some people can join, but for others the gap is too wide.

The most lovable part of a person is the part that loves and evidence that the artist is in some way a master lover offers a number of things. It not only teaches us new dimensions of love and reveals the artist as lovable, it also gives evidence that we ourselves, notwithstanding our many failures, may still be lovable and, therefore, still able to love. When one looks at a painting by Van Gogh, one sees a scene, perhaps a field of corn, as one has not seen one before. One sees that he saw in the field more than one habitually sees. This both opens the possibility that one's own appreciation of fields, and therefore of the world at large, may be enhanced, and allows us to appreciate the artist for his ability to esteem the field in the way that his painting gives evidence of. We shall also, of course, admire his skill in using his materials. All these three elements will enter into our act of appreciation. We shall not, however, want our perception of the last to dominate the other two. The skill of a great artist generally includes the ability to make great skill look easy, so that the skill itself becomes transparent rather than salient. Ideally, both the skill and the artist disappear and the artefact does its work directly.

When we talk of a bridge to the artist's inner world we do not mean that the art object necessarily is autobiographical in any way. Art does not have to be self-expression. Indeed, most good art is not self-directed and even when it is, as in a self-portrait, the self has to be distanced and become an object for the artistic purpose. It is not through self-description that the artist becomes known to us, but through the manner in which she treats of the objects and materials of her art. This is true irrespective of what type of art we are talking about. The principle applies as well to a painting as to a poem and although it may be less clear what the 'object' of a piece of music may be the problem in this respect is no greater than that of discerning sincerity or authenticity in a musical production, and, in any case, perhaps this supposed difficulty is actually more a reflection of modern views for does not "Aristotle repeatedly and most emphatically say that the most imitative of all Arts is Music, and that the *homoiomata* or likenesses produced by music are most exactly like the originals" (Murray p.79)? For Aristotle, music directly replicates emotion.

The suggestion that we are making here accounts for there being both a native response to art that does not need to be educated as well as for the change in appreciation that does come through education. Education provides a refinement of sensitivity that produces a shift in the art appreciator's understanding of what the artist is doing that may in turn change the appreciation of the work. The question of whether and in what way a work of art appreciates, esteems and renders sublime its objects is amenable to both a native and an educated response. In other words, if what we are doing when we look at art is in some way processing our understanding of love and experiencing love for the object world beyond the art object then we are likely to experience relevant feelings whether we have any 'art education' or not, but we may experience more feelings or more subtleties of understanding insofar as we do have such education. The uneducated eye and the educated are alike looking for sublimity, but the uneducated is more likely to see it in the inherent sublimity of the object and will want the artist to represent a sublime object with as little getting in the way as possible, that is, literalistically, whereas the more sophisticated observer appreciates more the transformative value of art that is not so immediately 'easy' but which invites us to see unpromising subject matter in new ways. Nonetheless, since part of the role of the artist is to expand our horizons of love, the artist must still rely upon eliciting the native response even in the educated since education, while it opens up understanding of what is known, is likely also to hold appreciation back in relation to what goes outside the tradition, since education always relates to a tradition.

The element of empathy for the artist, for his struggle and towards a feelingful understanding of what he is trying to do is part of this. We are suggesting that through art we re-esteem our world. The artist and the art object are catalyst elements in this transformation. However, with all this said, sincerity itself can hardly be a criterion of the art itself. Certainly if an artist concerns himself with such a matter that very concern will immediately start to corrode the art. Sincerity is not a quality that one can cultivate any more than one can plan spontaneity.

Art and Goodness

Iris Murdoch suggests that "art is an excellent analogy of morals, or indeed.... a case of morals. We cease to be in order to attend to the existence of something else, a natural object, a person in need. We can see in mediocre art... the intrusion of fantasy, the assertion of self" (Murdoch 1970, p.58). So good art grips us and takes us out of ourselves, especially out of the old habitual self that we otherwise take for granted. "It is not simply that suppression of self is required before accurate vision can be obtained. The great artist sees his objects (and this is true whether they are sad, absurd, repulsive or even evil) in a light of justice and mercy. The direction of attention is... outward, away from self which reduces all to a false unity, toward the great surprising variety of the world, and the ability so to direct attention is love." (*ibid*. p.65).

To this second passage we may add several points. Firstly, it is not that suppression of self is required before accurate vision becomes possible so much as that accurate vision dispels self and a role of art is to wake us up. The disappearance of self is thus not so much something to be undertaken as something that happens when one looks with loving and truthful eyes and   the work of the great artist facilitates this. In this sense art is therapeutic and the artist and therapist are engaged in similar tasks.

Secondly, Murdoch is saying that to see in the light of justice and mercy is to love and here justice does not mean something that has a capacity for condemnation, but something that is willing to find the justice in reality, which is to say, to find the lovable.

Thirdly, she here touches upon the kind of difficulty that can arise from ideas of oneness and unity. The supposed oneness of the universe may be nothing more than a projection since self is a desire for personal unification and completeness and leads to an understandable wish to see the world as unified and complete; or, to put the same thing a different way, since self arises upon the back of perception of the world and then generates its own (secondary) motives, those motives will include attempts to distort perception of the world in ways that keep the self intact (unitary) and, since self is substantially a mirror of what is seen, this leads to a (distorting) motive to see the world also as unitary and intact. 'Oneness' is a symptom of psychic fragility: if my self-concept is a reflection of my perception of others and I want to be a certain way then I must wish that they be so. Love, however, is a willingness to not impose oneself, but to appreciate the other just as they are.

Murdoch concludes, "It is in the capacity to love, that is to see, that the liberation of the soul from fantasy consists." Now here, by fantasy she does not mean the capacity of constructive imagination, but the self-serving distortions and indulgences of the ego. The important point to underline for our purpose is the equivalence between loving and truthful seeing: to truly see (or hear) another (as other) is to love them.

In as much as art "is a case of morals" we can see that morals are not to be equated with a fixed code since art is endlessly inventive and depends upon invention. An art object has to be new. Even if it is made in a style that is time honoured, it has to be a new instance of that style sufficiently distinctive to be attention catching so that one says, "And here is a superb example of...." The newness of the art object invites us to see anew, which is essential to the exercise. Art invites us to look anew and perceive what we have never discerned before. How is that moral? It is moral in reinvigorating the flow of love in our life. That is the moral thing to do.

This then is the moral compass of art and it is the artistic nature of morals. It shows morals not to be a dead conformity. This does not mean that a situation of 'anything for the sake of newness' is particularly valuable. Generally speaking, 'new' is only discernible in relation to a tradition, and art, therefore, even in this post-modern world, always sits in relation to a tradition, always misinterprets it, fails to understand its influence, in fact makes a 'misprision' of it (Bloom 1997), but, nonetheless cannot be understood without it. Language itself is tradition and within it there are innumerable traditions of usage. The same is true of the 'language' of paint, music, or any other art. The truly moral is correspondingly always a new act. The response that a therapist makes to a client, however much it may be formed or constrained by her tradition, be it person centred, analytic or whatever, must be new in this sense. It must be a work of art or it will be a dead thing and a dead thing alone cannot rouse the flow of love. The artist is exactly the same. His art must live.

Similarly, the tradition itself should be alive and is brought to life by the interpretation of it that is given by each artist, therapist or practitioner. This is what T.S.Eliot meant in his famous essay *Tradition and the Individual Talent* (Eliot 1932/1999). "The existing order is complete before the new work arrives; for order to persist after the supervention of novelty, the whole existing order must be, if ever so slightly, altered; and so the relations, proportions, values of each work of art toward the whole are readjusted; and this is conformity between the old and the new." (p.15). Eliot here gives a particular sense to tradition, something that can only be acquired by great application, as something that is remade by each creative act that occurs within it. This is very close to Buber's point that when we encounter a 'You', a love object, everything is then seen 'in it's light'. A genuine art object is such and casts such a light. To do this it must both stand within a tradition and be new. "To conform merely would be for the new work not really to conform at all; it would not be new, and would therefore not be a work of art" (*ibid*.) or, we might say, an act of love.

Art as Imitation
We have already noted that Aristotle saw music and all of what

he regarded as fine arts as imitation or replication (*mimesis*). This 'fine' category did not include architecture since architects did not make imitations, they made real things: real houses, temples and other buildings. This is a different classification from that common today. 'Imitation' tends now to be a word with a negative valence and it is not immediately obvious to a modern person how a replica can 'live'. Aristotle, however, saw that mimesis, the making of replicas, was capable of being one of the most important elements in a civilization. It will help us if we take time to understand this way of thinking. The function of the arts, Aristotle declared, was to delight. Arts may have other functions. A work of art may criticise society, may represent experimentation with its medium, may challenge the beholder in various ways, but all these, in the end, come down to variation upon the theme of delight. Delight can take many forms. We can understand immediately that delight is close to esteem. To provide delight is to help to esteem. We esteem what delights us. If an artist makes an 'imitation' that delights us then our quota of delight in life has increased.

If art is imitation, or we could say, representation, what is it that art imitates? One can easily see that some art is representational in an obvious way: a landscape painting, for instance. However, art is really operating at a deeper level than the camera. Murray, referring to Aristotle's analysis of poetry, says, "What objects does his poet imitate or make imitations of? 'Characters, emotions, and *praxeis*' - how shall we translate the last word? Most scholars translate 'actions'... but I cannot help thinking that Professor Margoliouth is right in taking it from... 'to fare', though in that case we have no exact noun to translate it by. Poetry shows the 'farings' of people, how they fare, well or ill. It is not confined to showing 'actions'." (Murray 1964, p.80). Poetry and all art creates replicas of how people are, how they experience life and how they fare so that in one way or another we can 'delight' in life. Now this fits our theory exactly. If art is designed to inspire us to delight in life, then it is to help us to love.

This does not mean that all objects of art are delightful in the simple sense. Indeed, it is often the special duty of art to enable us to find a kind of 'delight', often of the most intense sort, in precisely those things that are not obviously or originally delightful. This is why tragedy is regarded as a particularly high form of art. The delight that we get from comedy is trivial by comparison. Aristotle calls the figures that appear in tragedy 'good' even when they are villains, because they are high icons of culture the contemplation of which ultimately makes us into better people.

We do not become better, in this approach, by reasoning nor by obedience to moral codes, but by reconnecting with the spring of morals which is love. We become better as a result of what we contemplate and art aims to make us contemplate certain figures with intensity. This principle applies to all the modes that Aristotle calls 'imitative': poetry, music, painting, sculpting, dance and so on.

Esteem and Spirituality

Consider the following two stories related about the Japanese Buddhist sage Honen Shonin.

The Story of the Samurai Tadatsumi

The temple of Enryakuji was one of the largest and most powerful in Japan. In the tenth century it had started to appoint soldier monks to defend it. By the twelfth century it had become powerful enough to have become a threat to the civil authorities and declared a degree of independence from the secular government. The samurai Taro Tadatsumi was chosen by the emperor to lead a body of troops to put down the rebellion. In the autumn of 1192, just as he was about to set out to battle, Tadatsumi paid a visit to Honen. He told Honen that he had been moved by the latter's teaching that anybody who had faith and called upon the Buddha Amida would go to the Pure Land Paradise at death. However, he went on to say that he was responsible to the emperor, to his family and ancestors to do his duty on the battle field. "If I throw myself into driving back the enemy, all sorts of terrible and furious passions are likely to be stirred within me so that it becomes very hard to awaken any kind of spiritual feeling in my heart. If I allow myself to keep thinking all the time about the impermanence of life and try not to forget the truth about heaven by calling the Buddha's name then I'll be in danger of being taken prisoner by my enemies, being eternally branded as a coward and having my estate confiscated." He asks Honen what he should do.

Honen tells him that Amida Buddha loves people whether they are good or bad and will come to save a person who calls to him irrespective of how that person dies or what the circumstances of the person's life may have been. "So, even though a person born into an archer's family goes to war and loses his life, if he only repeats the sacred name and relies upon the Buddha's vow to save those who call upon him, there is not the slightest doubt that Amida will come to welcome him to the Pure Land."

Tadatsumi was greatly up-lifted by these words. Honen gave him a sacred scarf to wear under his armour. As he left the samurai said, "Tadatsumi's birth in the Pure Land will indeed take place today." Later the same day, Tadatsumi died in battle fighting against Enryakuji. A purple cloud appeared over the battlefield and people said that Tadatsumi had gone to the Pure Land Paradise. (Watts & Tomatsu 2005, pp. 34-35)

The Story of the Prostitute of Muro

In 1207 Honen was himself sent into exile. On the way to Shikoku the boat called in at the port of Muro. A small boat drew up alongside carrying a woman of the night who wanted to talk to Honen. She talked to him about the many sins that she had committed as part of her way of life. "What can a woman who carries a load of karma like mine do to escape and be saved in the world to come?"

Honen commented that her guilt was indeed surely great and the karmic consequences could be dire. He advised her that if she could find another means of livelihood to do so at once, but if she could not or was not yet ready to give up her present ways then she should simply start to call the name of the Buddha. "It is for just such deluded people as you that Amida Buddha made his wonderful all encompassing promise. So just put your faith in it fully."

Honen continued on his journey into exile. A year later he was pardoned. On his journey back the boat again called at Muro and Honen made enquiries about the woman who had come to see him. He found out that from the time she had visited him she had retired to a village near the mountains and devoted herself to the practice of calling the Buddha's name. After some time she had died peacefully and the signs indicated her rebirth in heaven. (Watts & Tomatsu 2005, pp.50-51).

I would like to look at these two stories from the perspective of esteem theory. What I want to look at is the attitude and actions of Honen in each case. He does not give the same response to each. In the case of the samurai, Honen can see that the soldier is going to go to battle whatever he says. Honen might be a gentle Buddhist priest who has given up all forms of combat, but here before him is a man at arms on the way to the battlefield. The man is frightened that he is worthless and doomed. He may well die in the battle, but will he die in a state of despair and bitterness? Honen's responses ensure that he does not. Tadatsumi makes a good death, even though he has been a killer. Honen does not hesitate to help him in this way. Honen sees what is of value in the man. He sees his loyalty and commitment. He sees the faith that the samurai does have which has been at least suffi-cient to cause him to make the visit to Honen in the first place. There is nothing in Honen's response to him that shows an ounce of disapproval notwithstanding the fact that Honen had come into the Buddhist priesthood following the assassination of his own father by an archer in many ways similar to Tadatsumi.

In the case of the prostitute, Honen does suggest that she might change her career. He senses that she may be at a stage where she would be willing to give it up. He does not press the point and offers her also a way that does not involve renouncing her profession. This creates a situation where it is entirely her choice, but he has given a slight push in the direction of a more sober life. In modern language we might say that he is not totally non-directive. This is, however, just the added impetus that the woman needs to make the change. She finds a village near the mountains that she can retire to and takes to the religious life, ending her spell on this earth in peace.

Both the warrior and the prostitute live in a society in which the idea of going to the Pure Land or to hell or of being reborn in this world according to your karma is a backdrop to everyone's life. Honen, and everything he says, is within this tradition. At some point the characters of our two stories who consulted Honen each realised the lives they were living were incompatible with the traditional religious teaching. By living in a sinful way they were piling up bad karma and in principle doomed. A more conventional teacher than Honen might well have told each of them that it was vitally important that they change their ways immediately and adopt some spiritual practice that he could indicate for them. In other words, the conventional teacher would have responded in a way that took morality to be a code, yet, in doing so he would have underlined what was unlovable in each of them. We can sense that Honen, by contrast, had already found ways to love each of them. In each case the way of doing so is different, but the basic act in each case is to see what still is lovable and love it. His response therefore 'lives' in each case. It is artistic. That is surely why both supplicants went away feeling elevated. Not just that they felt loved, but that faith in the possibility of love even in a world as defeating as this was restored for them.

Sustaining Love

Spiritual paths provide means whereby a person may continue to believe in love even when the odds are heavily stacked against. If, like Honen Shonin, one believes that Amida Buddha does not judge anybody but continues to love people irrespective of what sort of life they have lived then it is easier to go on finding the lovable aspect of each person and each situation that arises. Parallel ideas can be found in many spiritual traditions.

Most people are familiar with the refrain "All's well and all shall be well, all manner of things shall be well." This was a teaching revealed by Jesus Christ to the anchoress Julian of Norwich during a vision. Julian was, incidentally, the first woman ever to write a book in the English language. The book is called *Revelations of Divine Love* (Julian 1901). Julian's vision is of Christ crucified. She sees all his suffering in vivid detail. She also is herself troubled by the thought of sin that comes between people and God and impedes the holy life. However, Jesus says to her, "Synne is behovabil, but al shal be wel & al shal be wel & al manner of thyng shal be wel." That is, sin happens, but all shall be well anyway. Julian sees that God's love is not impeded by sin. "He blameth not me for sin" (p.57). She is saying that a truly loving God will love irrespective of whether the creature is sinning or not. In fact, since it is in the nature of beings to sin, their sinning nature has to be part of their lovability.

Iris Murdoch offers a simple way of relating spirituality to our theme when she says that "Prayer is properly not petition, but simply an attention to God which is a form of love." (Murdoch 1970, p. 53-54). She points out that God is a focus for attention, that such focus provides energy, and that when such a focus is strong as in the case of falling in love, the will is more or less powerless against it. "Deliberately falling out of love is not a jump of the will, it is the acquiring of new objects of attention." (*ibid*. p.54) and "We can all receive moral help by focussing our attention upon things which are valuable: virtuous people, great art, perhaps... the idea of goodness itself" and "our ability to act well 'when the time comes' depends partly, perhaps largely, upon the quality of our habitual objects of attention." (p.55). We can say, therefore, that spirituality has much to do with habits of perception and particularly perception of what is good; and what is best is love itself. There is a circularity in all this as there should be. It is loving to look upon what is lovable and to do so in a loving way and looking upon what is lovable itself fosters love. The highest concepts and figures of religion embody these virtues. To relate to God or Buddha is to relate to goodness and love and thereby to become more loving. There is a parallel between the transcendent and the mundane. To look at features of the mundane world in a loving way, to see what it is in them that is lovable, is both healing for them and healing for the looker. It is worship. It might be expressed in such phrases as "seeing that of God in every man." There is a danger when this kind of idea gets translated into a metaphysic (i.e. codified) that it is in some degree reified, for then a person might reason that if God is in every man then He is in oneself and become self-focussed in consequence. This, however, will not work: "the direction of attention should be outward, away from self" (*ibid*. p.58).

Love as Moral Progress

Non-arrival: Progress Toward Perfect Love

Iris Murdoch in her essay *The Sovereignty of Good* considers a case of a mother and daughter-in-law where in the first stage the mother acts very properly toward the daughter-in-law, but, nonetheless, inwardly scorns her, believing that her son has married beneath himself, yet, over time, the mother reconsiders and gradually comes to appreciate the good features of the daughter-in-law, perhaps starting to see in her what her son saw, and arrives at a new attitude, more highly esteeming than before, but still continues throughout to act in the same proper way toward her. The daughter-in-law, for her part, never gets to know of these changes of attitude in the mother. Murdoch suggests that the mother has here engaged in a moral process even though there is no change in her behaviour. She has become more loving even though she does not act in a changed way. The force of the example might, she suggests, be increased if we imagine that the daughter-in-law lives abroad or even has died. The point is that the change in the mother is wholly inward, is moral and is to do with love. I read this passage, though not for the first time, after I had started writing this book and immediately recognised that it fits very well with the proposition being advanced here. What changes is also, crucially, the mother's perception of the daughter-in-law. Thus Murdoch writes, "Moral change and moral achievement are slow; we are not free in the sense of being able suddenly to alter ourselves since we cannot suddenly alter what we can see and ergo what we desire and are compelled by. In a way, explicit choice seems now less important, less decisive (since much of the 'decision' lies elsewhere) and less obviously something to be 'cultivated'. If I attend properly I will have no choices and this is the ultimate condition to be aimed at. This is in a way the reverse of.... increasing our freedom by conceptualizing as many different possibilities of action as possible: having as many goods as possible in the shop. The ideal situation, on the contrary, is rather to be represented as a kind of 'necessity'. This is something of which saints speak and which any artist will readily understand. The idea of a patient, loving regard, directed upon a person, a thing, a situation, presents the will not as unimpeded movement but as something very much more like 'obedience'."(Murdoch 1970, pp.38-39).

Murdoch is pointing out that the will follows perception, and, in particular follows that special form of perception that we are here calling esteem, and further that esteem is the making of love. As M's esteem for D grows so does her love. This love is an internal attribute in the sense that it is something known and felt by M that does not appear in her behaviour, but it is a function of her regard for an other, namely D. Murdoch uses this example it refute the idea that morality has to be action.

The human organism is not a thing unto itself only, and only becomes a thing unto itself as a secondary formation. Primarily to looks outward. Murdoch also concurs that this esteem is what love is made of and that it is, therefore, moral, and the making of what is moral. She also points out that this has the further implications that moral change, which is the growth of love, is slow since it is inherently a change of perception and changes in perception do not generally come in big leaps, and, associated with this, she introduces the notion that we are talking about a process that in concept points toward perfection, but a perfection never attained, and that this in turn implies *de facto* imperfection. "M's activity is essentially something progressive, something infinitely perfectible. So far from claiming for it a sort of infallibility, this new picture has built in the notion of a necessary fallibility. M is engaged in an endless task. As soon as we begin to use words such as 'love' and 'justice' in characterizing M, we introduce into our whole conceptual picture of her situation the idea of progress, that is the idea of perfection" (Murdoch 1970. p.23). This point is surely enormously important. If what is truly moral is the progress of love, then we are no longer talking about justification in a black and white manner. Where a court of law has to decide 'innocent' or 'guilty', the court of life is quite different. Here we are always on a journey. "Man is not a combination of an impersonal rational thinker and a personal will. He is a unified being who sees, and who desires in accordance with what he sees, and who has some continual slight control over the direction and focus of his vision. There is nothing, I think, in the foreground of this picture which is unfamiliar to the ordinary person." (*ibid*. p.39).

Murdoch also claims that "The idea of perfection moves, and possibly changes, us (as artist, worker, agent) because it inspires love in the part of us that is most worthy." (*ibid*. p.60). Here she is relying upon the principle, as we would put it, that, love being esteem, to gaze upon (whether with the mind's eye or the literal one) what is most highly esteemed (which perfection is, by definition) is generative of love. The type of love depends upon the context and type of perfection. Thus, a craftsman may be moved by the idea of perfection in his craft (in the mind's eye) or by a tangible masterpiece (the literal eye). The craftsman will be even more moved than the non-specialist by an example of near-perfection, as the craftsman is somebody who particularly esteems and understands the value of such work, say, it might be woodcarving, and when we here say 'understands' we are not talking about a primarily cognitive function, though it will have cognitive dimensions. Nor need we think that the craftsman's transport of delight in seeing a masterpiece of his own trade is due to a projection of his self or an identification. To think so would certainly demean the whole idea and miss the experiential reality for the man. Imagine yourself into the position of the wood carver. He sets eyes upon a piece of work that is exquisite. He gasps in awe. That is a transcendent moment. Elements of self might creep in afterwards, such as 'I wish I could make one of those,' 'I wonder what that is worth,' and so on, but they detract. In the initial purity of response there is no 'self' and only delight. It is a moment of love. Whether such a moment is classifiable as art or religion is not determinable. It is both. It is love.

Thus Murdoch continues, "great art teaches us how real things can be looked at and loved without being seized and used, without being appropriated into the greedy organism of the self... in moral situations a similar exactness is called for." (Murdoch 1970, p. 64).

Singularity of the Love Object

Love, as we discussed in Part Two, involves selection. Does this pose a moral problem? Robert Ehman thinks that it does. He says, "The fundamental requirement of love is to raise the beloved above others" while "The fundamental requirement of morality in contrast is to treat all persons as having equal worth" (Ehman 1968, p.260). He goes on to describe the difficulties that arise when love and morality (as he defines them) come into conflict. He adds, "Love... cares nothing for general principles and fairness... For morality, on the other hand, the individual in his mere individuality is incidental" and, therefore, "the lover... cannot be counted on to act on moral principles even when he is a man of sound moral character." (*ibid.*)

Now this is a strong claim. Is it correct? I think it is only correct if we take moral to mean (as he does) the kind of codified morality that follows principles. I do not agree that the lover is morally unreliable as a result of loving. I suspect that Murdoch would have agreed with me. A good deal here turns on what we think the nature of morality is. It appears that for Ehman, morality means adhering to principles and that among those principles will be a principle of equality. This is, of course, in keeping with modern democratic thinking, but how long has democratic thinking been prevalent? Ehman would probably claim that the equality principle predates democratic politics and say that it is inherent in all great codes of morality back to Moses, Buddha and Zoroaster. It might be true of the codes, but, we should ask, is morality the same thing as the codes? Are not moral codes signposts toward morality rather than the thing itself? I think there is a fallacy here. I think that the fallacy lies in thinking that morality requires us to treat all the same. This is similar to the muddles that can arise around the idea of justice. Some (perhaps Murdoch is an example) seem to use the term justice to mean appreciation of what is good in people while others use it to mean the rules governing who is to be justified and who condemned. Many social movements call for justice while those in power claim that justice is what they administer. The two voices do not hear each other because they are using the same word to mean two different things. Ehman would mean, I suspect, equal treatment. However, is it moral to treat everybody the same? Certainly not in a simplistic sense. If I give two friends the same gift, an item that one had longed for and that the other regarded with distain, have I really treated them the same? Definitely not. So the superficial case does not work. However, if that is the case, then how am I to treat my friends 'the same'? Surely, I have got to know each of them with some intimacy. Let us assume that I do so know them. What will happen then? Shall I treat them equally? It is hardly likely. It is quite possible that I shall do (perhaps many) good things for each of them, but the idea of treating them equally is not likely to loom large in my mind and, in any case, as my knowledge of each of them becomes more total (and I am not just talking about accumulation of information about them) the notion of 'treating them the same' actually becomes less and less meaningful. This is because the more that each becomes a real friend, the more unique they become and the more it becomes the case that when I think of one friend that one commands my full attention. This is, I think, what Buber is also getting at: "Every actual relationship to another being in the world is exclusive. Its You is freed and steps forth to confront us in its uniqueness. It fills the firmament - not as if there were nothing else, but everything else lives in its light. As long as the presence of the relationship endures, this world-wideness cannot be infringed. But as soon as a You becomes an It, the world-wideness of the relationship appears as an injustice against the world, and its exclusiveness as an exclusion of the universe." (Buber p.126-127). So Buber, like Ehman, also talks about exclusiveness, but in a different way. In Buber, all love objects are exclusive *at the time that one regards them.*

I think that Ehman is making too strong a distinction between different kinds of love. He singles out the love that a person has for one unique person in their life, but I prefer to maintain that love is not like that. Love is expressed through many relationships, and not just with people. Is this not so? We therefore are using the concept differently and, perhaps, as with the different usages of 'justice' mentioned earlier, missing each other. It may be that I am doing an injustice to Ehman, but whether this is the case or not, he has led me to try to clarify the matter in terms of an other centred approach, in which there is love and there are many others. I can esteem many friends. Doing so each of them takes on a 'supreme and wondrous value' (Ehman's term), but the fact that each is supreme in its own way does not preclude the others from each also being supreme. Each is a supreme case of what it is. Love is a matter of seeing the other as a unique and supreme case of exactly what it is (whereas equality contains a notion of denial of uniqueness). Insofar as one does so discern, one loves. One love does not necessarily preclude others. Indeed, one of the ways that we express our love is by sharing the things we love with our beloved.

What then of the special love that one may have for a spouse, which is what Ehman is concerned about? Firstly it is obvious that the fact that one has a spouse does not preclude one loving parents, friends, or children. Yet, each of these loves would, presumably, also have the capacity to render a person 'morally unreliable' in Ehman's sense. Indeed, love for children might be even stronger in this regard. We, therefore, have to ask, is that really immoral? Is it not moral to treat one's children as special? Surely it is. Indeed, is it actually moral to treat anybody 'the same as everybody else' if you know that person closely? I think not. Treating people all the same is only moral, surely, when one does not know those people. When you do not know people as individuals, as I do not know the people of a town in Siberia, say, then it is probably the most loving thing that I can do to put them on a par in my mind with people from anywhere else in the world. Yet, even at this point we must hesitate. Even this is not really right. If we so much as know that they live in a town in Siberia, then we know something. If we are going to treat them lovingly we shall take into account whatever it is that we do know. It is exactly this taking care over the individuality of the case that makes our regard one of love and not one of mechanical procedure. It is machines that treat people equally and that is not love; and it is love that is moral. Machines are not moral agents even though they might be able to follow a code. Human machines, such as bureaucracies, likewise. In ordinary human usage, equality and love point in different directions. They are only unified in the mind (or heart) of an ideal being (God or Buddha).

This reflection then makes us pause and ask whether the idea of treating 'all the same' is moral at all. Is not treating people all the same what we expect of the 'machinery' of state rather than the living being of other persons? Is not the importation of principles that are proper to social administration into our individual lives a process of demoralisation and is this not a widely disseminated folly? Could this be one of the reasons why modern life seems lacking in moral substance and conducive to anomie? Anomie is that state in which nothing matters particularly. Anomie is proper to machines, but not to people. Where anomie were established as the supreme value then it would indeed by immoral to treat one's beloved as special, but this is surely the up-ending of true values; and do we not see too much of it in our contemporary world?

A further derivative thought is that what Buber is saying about relationships applies equally well to relationships with art objects. The power of a great piece of art is surely exactly this, that it evokes, in the time of our encounter with it, precisely the kind of encompassing priority that he is referring to. At the time we see the whole world in its light. The universe is reconfigured around a new point of vantage which is the summit of that particular love. This does not come about because the artist has ensnared us by his technique. If he has tried to do so without there being congruence between technique and substance then technique has become mere ornamentation (Coombes 1953). It has come about as a function of the smooth and consummate integration of good technique with good meaningfulness on the part of the artist and by 'good' meaningfulness here we mean that the artist is expressing a particularly forceful esteem, flowing from his own grappling with the issues of love and its frustration that are our main theme.

Further, just as this is true of a work of art, so it is true of the special moments of therapy. I am inclined to understand the times when therapy reaches a peak of intensity as those times when the client becomes, in Buber's language, a You (Thou) rather than an It. Rogers understands those as times when one is closest to oneself, and, in his schema this makes sense, but what Rogers conceptualises as the times of closeness to one's own self are actually the times when he is most deeply engrossed in relationship. He refers to this as a "slightly altered state of consciousness" (Rogers 1980, p.129). He refers to the work of Grof (1977) and of Lilly (1973) on altered states using the term "transcending experience of unity" (*ibid*. p.128).

Now both the idea of closeness to one's 'inner intuitive self' (Rogers) and that of 'transcendent unity' (Grof) do provide a language that gives a means to speak about this condition, but it is a condition in which the most powerful phenomenological element is actually the other, not the self. I do not think that even Rogers is saying that the 'self' is here experienced as in any sense an entity and he is certainly referring to those times when he becomes closest to, or, let us be even more precise, most overwhelmingly attentive to, an other. When Rogers talks of 'presence' he is talking about presence to an other and he does not mean to put the emphasis upon what the other perceives of him so much as upon what happens to him when he perceives the other. It seems to me, therefore, that the language of 'self' and 'presence', while not totally unworkable, is, in this context, not the most apt. What is being talked about is those times when an other becomes a 'supreme and wondrous value', and this interpretation of Rogers and description of the actual phenomenology of the encounter situation is wholly in keeping with Rogers' central focus upon it being 'client centred therapy' and upon the vital importance of listening and attending in a fully congruent way. I do not, therefore, think that I am here refuting the substance of what Rogers is saying, but rather providing a more appropriate way of expressing that substance and this different way of expressing it has the advantage of showing how Rogers' earliest principles and discoveries are still central to his later conclusions as well as making simpler and more direct sense of what is going on.

Rather similar considerations apply to the idea of 'transcendent unity'. It is a workable terminology up to a point, but, as a matter of phenomenology, one does not unify with the other; one regards, listens to and possibly stands in awe of the other. The other does not become self. There is some sense in the idea that in such moments one 'loses oneself', but that does not imply unity with the other or the other's unity with oneself, merely that self-consciousness sometimes ceases at such times. I do not think that it is a criterion of such times that it do so, though there might be a particular satisfaction in it doing so, if one can speak of 'satisfaction' without self-consciousness. One does not at such moments obliterate the mystery of the other. They remain other. Their otherness is in fact a most powerful ingredient of such a situation. It is in their otherness that fascination resides. If we really did merge there would be nothing remaining to make the matter notable. No. What such expressions as 'transcendent unity' and Rogers' 'presence' refer to are times when the other becomes a 'supreme and wondrous value'.

As soon as we start to understand the matter in these terms we can immediately appreciate the common ground with what is happening in art. When a client tells his story it is really not so different to watching a piece of theatre and there are times in such theatre when one becomes completely rapt, when the whole thing matters and comes alive. At such times, which may be long or short lived, we are affected by the other in a way that is not just a superficial experience. We are changed, or, more immediately, our world reconstellates. It is the presence of the other both in their manifest character and in the mystery of what remains hidden that at such a point becomes of supreme importance. Both the element of manifestation and of mystery are essential to this.

Love, therefore, is not a matter of making one love object supreme at the expense of all others, even though love may sometimes result in conflicts as we have seen, and this is true even when one has a prime love object such as a spouse. It is a matter of making every object that is a love object supreme in its sphere. The spouse has a particular sphere and in that sphere is supreme, but this does not eliminate the spheres of children, parents, or indeed waterfalls and sunsets.

Happiness is Not the Goal

There is currently a good deal of concern with the attainment of happiness. Happiness research is popular, but tends to show that the happiness quotient of individuals does not actually vary much over the lifespan. The idea of happiness development has been given a particular lift by the suggestion by the former King of Bhutan that gross national happiness might be a better indicator than gross national product for assessing how well a country is doing or how well a government serves its people. Gross national product is certainly an unsatisfactory measure for many reasons, economic as well as ethical, but the components of an index of national happiness are also likely to be highly subjective so this is soft science at best. There is certainly some value in the advance of ideas like gross national happiness or gross international happiness that have grown out of values found in Buddhist philosophy among other sources. These kinds of ideas can certainly stimulate and spur those who would like to see forms of development that are less centred on money-making and they do lead one to question what is really important in all forms of therapy, whether therapy for the individual or, as development may be seen, therapy for nations or even the planet.

Nonetheless, there are pitfalls in putting happiness centre stage. Among other things, to love is undoubtedly to wish that the other be happy, including the sub-ordinate wishes that the other be freed from particular sources of pain and misery and that they receive or be endowed with benefits and graces. However, love is not ended or fulfilled in some final way when such benefits arrive nor is it destroyed when they fail to appear. Further, love has deeper levels. One might at one and the same time wish that one's child be spared hardship and wish that they have such adventures as may lead them to become a strong character, and the incompatibility of these two aspects of true love is a common source of anxiety for parents.

An other centred approach, therefore, while acknowledging that love seeks happiness for the other, does not see happiness itself as the goal of life. John Shlien puts this well when he says, "If happiness is at all a consequence, it is not a direct consequence of therapy. Therapy does not make happiness. The client may create happiness, as a secondary effect. In spite of its seeming to be of ultimate significance, it is not an end-product in itself but a by-product of other positive factors, much as confidence, self-esteem, *accomplishments*, etc.... happiness is not a valid end-in-itself or end-by-itself. If it comes, it is not only a consequence of other factors, but it will be *one consequence among many*. Whatever enables happiness will also enable a wide range of other experiences, such as sadness, loneliness, or whatever life may bring. What therapy makes is the *capacity* for happiness, not the happiness itself." (Shlien 2003, pp.71-72, original italics).

Love enhances life and life involves diverse experience. Love also makes one care about the fate of others and thus inevitably entrains grief. One cannot love without suffering as a consequence and while a loving life does yield much happiness, as Shlien points out, it yields other things too and that is why life is colourful and not monochrome and why there is both psychopathology and character development. "The one thing therapy does not bring is indifference, or numbness. It brings sensitivity. You can smell the new-cut grass in summer - also the garbage". (*ibid*. p.76).

The Question of Tragedy

We need to think now of why and how it can be 'delightful' to observe on the stage or in other artistically depicted scenes, events or circumstances that are inherently distressing. As we do so we can keep in mind the ever-present parallel between art and therapy. The therapist spends much of her time being a witness to the client's depiction of such matters. Sometimes what the client says may seem heart-breaking, yet the therapist may count those moments amongst the most memorable as times when the relationship with the client became most powerful and rewarding. This is not to say that there should be any premium in therapy upon elicitation of such scenes, but there can be no doubt that the times when the client reveals matters that have taken them to the edge of their humanity are of particular force and do not, in general, have the effect of undermining, but of strengthening both the therapist's esteem for the client and the therapist's satisfaction in the performance of the professional role. We cannot regard this as in any way a form of sadistic pleasure. It is evidently quite otherwise. Already, we have to admit that there is a kind of delight; not the kind of delight that is associated with levity, but something altogether more serious.

Aristotle saw tragedy as theatre depicting incidents arousing pity and fear, through which the audience arrive at a catharsis, especially of those emotions. Tragedy is mimesis of how things fare according to some form of necessity. In a tragedy we see how a chain of events unfolds from beginnings. We see how things that were not wished for come about inexorably from the commitments, often mistaken or unwise, of the leading characters. For Aristotle, tragedy is drama rather than narrative; it 'shows' rather than 'recounts'. Whereas history tells us what happened in actuality, tragedy, even when it is based on a true story, is finer than history because it deals with the universal case. Tragedy thus has universal relevance. History may lead us to doubt that the laws of the universe still function or that the gods still have sway, but tragedy shows us how they function all too well and how the gods are very much still in business and while this is terrible it is also reassuring at a deeper level. If the gods still live then there is still love in the world, notwithstanding circumstantial evidence in the world, or on the stage, or in the life of the client to the contrary. The effect of tragedy, therefore, is to raise us to a higher plain, to a vantage point where we get a glimpse as from the gods, and this takes our breath away, frightens us, moves us to pity, but finally leaves us with the most profound kind of delight which is the delight that we take in being part of an order that is greater and more mighty than anything that we ourselves could devise or control. Herein lies the secret of the restoration of love when all seems to have been laid waste.

Part Four:
Developing Theory and Practice

Love and Different Kinds of Esteem

In this essay so far I have used the word love in a manner that is very close to common usage. Some of the uses to which the word love is put seem, philosophically, to be difficult to reconcile with one another, but they speak of a basic human intuition. I have also taken it that to love is to esteem. What we love we hold dear. The manner and modes in which we do so may vary widely, but the basic proposition generally holds.

Thus object esteem can take many forms. The person who says that he loves salmon may mean that he devotes his life to saving their lives and preserving their habitats or he may mean that he likes to eat them. Or it might be the voice of a chef who thinks that the sight of that distinctive flesh laid out on a platter contributes a particular glory to his art. All three instances are examples of esteem of the salmon object and all are species of love even though they may speak of different ethics or aesthetics. We can see common ground here between things that from other perspectives would be dissimilar.

Thus to say that love is a core drive does not imply a particular ethical code. Love can take innumerable forms. The love of one thing generally implies actions that cause harm to other things. We live in a world where it is impossible to make omelettes without breaking eggs and even though making somebody an omelette may be a way of expressing love for them it also involves the use of eggs that were once living entities that could have become chickens. Had one's love been focussed upon the chickens instead, perhaps one would have acted differently. However, there is probably no love object within this world that one can serve without destructive effect on some other which may in part explain why humans have arrived at religions that posit a love object wholly beyond this world as the only way of being in touch with a love that is perfect and not compromised by the existential situation, a strategy that, in one way or another, seems to be vital to human sanity. Living in a confusing world we crave a reliable direction and are greatly aided by finding at least approximations to one.

Broadly we can say that a healthy life is one in which the need to love is being satisfied in some way, which is to say one in which the person has love objects that are not wholly frustrating. These love objects include what in many approaches to psychology are called 'significant others'. They also come to include the objects that hold one's attention through the process of sublimation. Some of the latter may be abstract objects such as country or profession. As one matures one also finds a portion of one's love increasingly channelled into pathways that serve the communal good rather than the good of the known individuals that one finds within one's family.

These communal love objects are symbolised in various ways. The adult person may in fact find that one of the most powerful dynamics in his or her life is presented by the conflicting demands of different love objects among which the symbolic objects of communal life play a major part. One might say that to love one's work is not the same thing as to love one's children, but although there is an obvious distinction they are both forms of love and both offer the satisfactions and frustrations that arise through loving. They also compete and co-operate with one another in the course of real life. None of these ideas is distant from what is immediately recognisable to the ordinary person in the street. One contention of this book is that by assuming love to be the basic driving force of human life it is possible to formulate many psychological phenomena in a manner that is immediately recognisable in the vernacular of ordinary people. This is an advantage in itself. If the language of the professional is not too removed from the language of the street unnecessary barriers to communication and understanding disappear. Everybody knows what it means for a person to love their work and what it means for them not to do so and we all recognise the resulting conflicts in our own families.

Expression of Love in a Tradition

Earlier I referred to Murdoch's demonstration that love may be found, may exist and may grow and change without ever being expressed. It seems important to keep this in mind. It provides a useful antidote to the strong winds of empiricism that tend to blow through our modern theorising and tell us sometimes, rather absurdly, that we did not think something if that thought never emerged as an action and so on. There has been a tendency to import the ways of physical science into psychology that create demands for everything to be measurable, at least in principle, when we all know from personal experience that many are not. Carl Rogers spent many hours devising ways of trying to measure the qualities that he was interested in and looked for what are now called 'performance indicators' that, as it were, give them away. Although this kind of quantitative method can be very useful in psychology at an indicative level, it can never (some might say, 'unfortunately') be definitive precisely because it does measure 'indicators' and not the thing itself to which the indicator has a necessarily erratic relation. In the arts the problem is even more fraught. It is a fallacy to think that measurement of something that is commonly associated with a phenomenon is measurement of the phenomenon itself.

All that said, generally love issues in expression and expression is interpreted, often most significantly by the love object, and the art of interpretation turns upon the background provided by a tradition. To put this otherwise, everything we do can be considered as communication and whoever is in receipt of communication tries to decipher it. One of the things they are looking for is indicators of love of various kinds. How they interpret what they see or hear is a function of two broad sets of factors: on the one hand, what was actually said and done, and on the other the social context (tradition) in which it occurred. To be hugged on arriving at a beach party in California is not at all the same thing as being hugged on arriving at the House of Lords. Now this is important because when we discuss 'technique' in psychotherapy, we are often talking about rituals considered out of their context.

Thus, it is entirely possible that one could interpret Rogers' basic theory in the following way: 'empathic response is the manner in which a therapist traditionally shows love to a client within the bounds of the psychotherapy relationship (where hugs and kisses might be taboo, for instance) and if you offer that authentically (which is what unconditional positive regard and congruence prescribe) then all will be well.' If he were taken in this way, it would immediately open up the possibility that there could be any number of other ways that a therapist could also show love within the bounds of the psychotherapy relationship. One immediately starts to think of the sorts of things that therapists from other schools of psychotherapy do such as devising behavioural programmes with the client, analysing complexes, searching for cognitive restructure, and so on. If one thinks in such a way, technique does not become useless, but it does start to be seen in a particular light. Perhaps in some circumstances what might express the appropriate kind of love would be to play hide and seek around the clinic building or go for a walk together and so on. We start to wonder if the narrowness of the range of psychotherapeutic technique does not have more to do with the dangers of expressing love too strongly in a manner that could be misinterpreted than with the particular efficacy of, say, the empathic understanding response. It may be more a case of that being one of the few things that a therapist is still allowed to do, than that that is a particularly powerful method in itself.

Nonetheless, the restrictions imposed by the rules and traditions do themselves have an effect. They add intensity. This is perhaps in some ways similar to the manner in which chivalric manners added intensity to romanticism. The more inaccessible the lady was, the more powerfully the passion for her could develop. While Rogers believes that transference is minimised in his approach by the therapist's willingness to be available 'as herself', and he is partly right, it must surely also be the case that the sheer fact that therapist and client cannot do together many of the things that in the culture at large friends or lovers do, adds intensity and fuels fantasy. We shall come back to the question of transference later. Here I want to concentrate on the technique half of the equation.

The suggestion here is that technique is contextual and lacks primary significance, except in the mechanical domain. By this last phrase, I mean that if you teach a client how to relax, that is a technique that he can take away and use without reference to you. That kind of technique has a circumscribed utility that may be of intrinsic worth to a client, just as a piece of information (such as the phone number of the Housing Department) may be. That kind of thing is, however, peripheral to psychotherapy *qua* therapy. It is useful but in itself does not heal the soul. What heals the soul is a change in a person's capacity to esteem their world. The therapist relates to the client as an esteemed other, but it is the manner in which the client relates to the significant others in his own world that finally determines his faring and his fate.

Object Relations

The Client's Natural Flow
In the initial setting out of esteem theory at the beginning of this book, I said that the manner in which people esteem objects is a prime symptom of the functioning of the strong and weak drives.

This is why the client's process of perception is such an important focus of attention for the therapist. The therapist needs to know how the client sees things. That more than anything else tells us what we need to know about the client's psychological state. It is still a kind of 'performance indicator' in that it indicates to us the movements of love within the client's heart that we shall never perceive directly, but it is usually a critically important one. The other person will always be a mystery in the matter of love as that is what it is to be a person, but still, if we can understand that person's manner of perceiving the significant things in their world we shall have one of the most important indicators.

Firstly, to what extent is the client capable of seeing things and secondly in what way does he or she perceive them? Perception inherently involves evaluation. We are therefore always enquiring into the process of esteem. How does the client esteem his world globally and the individual significant others within it? Does she have objects of esteem, what are they, in what way does she esteem them, what does she not hold in esteem, how, why? These kinds of questions tell us much about who and what a person is, what their life consists of and what it means.

So strong has the concern with the self become in our psychological professions and in our society generally, however, that many therapists see this kind of data as no more important than secondary evidence of how the person perceives self. Other centred theory reverses this evaluation. It is self that is the secondary formation and object regard that is primary.

Let us consider a stereotypical session with a new client. The client comes to the therapist who invites the client to tell their story. The client does so. If the client does not have previous experience of therapy and has not immersed himself in popular psychology books then it is quite likely that the inexperienced client's story will have little if any reference to self (though with the growing penetration of self psychology ideas into popular media this is changing). The story will be a parade of the significant others in the client's life. He will tell the therapist who they are and, especially, what they did and said. The therapist might even have difficulty keeping track of who is who. Now therapists of many different psychological schools are likely before long to intervene in this natural flow of client consciousness with a remark that in one way or another says, "And how is this for you?". In other words, the therapist directs the client to stop talking about others and redirect attention to the self. This type of intervention is extremely common even among therapists who believe in non-directivity. The typical therapist is so convinced of the centrality of self-regard to the therapy process that he is blind to the fact that drawing the client's attention to it is a directive intervention that takes the client out of their natural flow. Further, many therapists would not know what to do with the material that the client produces if the client only talks about others, even though it is that material that most immediately demonstrates the client in process. Therapy technique has in many cases become highly focussed upon self-examination. Issues of self-esteem, self-regard, self-evaluation and self-assertion have become paramount. The suggestion of other centred therapy is that all of this may be inappropriate.

By directing the client away from other-regard toward self-regard the therapist not only breaks the client's natural flow, she also takes the client into a domain that is full of secondary psychological constructions. These constructions are full of fear and pain and that is one reason why the therapist may believe that they are the area to examine, but that pain and fear has its origin in real encounters with real people and it represents the difficulty that the client has and has had in such encounters. A self psychology approach, even a supposedly non-directive one, risks miring the client in unnecessary abstraction and selling to him an ideology of self-entitlement that will not serve him.

The Self is a Function of Other-Regard

By treating self as secondary, just as the weak force of self-protection is secondary to the strong force of the need to reach out in love toward the world, therapy is reframed in a constructive manner that inherently values the most healthy and constructive elements in the client's life which are to do with positive engagement with the real world. Therapy does not have to be a process of deconstruction of pathology. It can be a directly constructive process of appreciation of what is healthy reinforcing the multitudinous expressions of love that already function in the client no matter how starved or stunted they may have become.

The manner in which self material is secondary can be understood by a simple consideration. Much therapy is concerned with a client's experience of fear. How does fear arise? Fear arises in relation to and in dependence upon a fearsome object. If a person sees a tiger at close quarters, or snake, that person experiences fear. To do so is normal, appropriate and healthy. In passing we can note that it is not, therefore, appropriate for therapy to have as a goal the complete elimination of fear from a person's life. Fear has its place. Its place is in response to a fearsome object. If you want to see a client's fear appear before you in the consulting room you have only got to have that client call to mind whatever it is that constitutes the fearsome object for them. If a client, even in fantasy, enters into the room where they were abused or humiliated, it is probable that they will experience fear. As the client visualises the scene the therapist will observe the client's pallor and muscle-tone change. If you need to see the client's fear this is a far more effective and direct route than inviting the client to talk about his fear. When he does so it becomes fear in the abstract, a secondary phenomenon, part of the self, but not part of real life. What you will see in this latter case is not the fear, but the constructions that the client has made in order to respond to fear. You may see his defences but you will not see his naked being and you will not persuade him to reconfigure those defences unless he discerns that you appreciate why they are as they are.

Consciousness is always consciousness of something. The mind is conditioned by its objects (Brazier, 1995, p 95 *et seq.*). All adventitious attributes of consciousness like fear arise according to what the object of consciousness is at the time. When the therapist asks the client to talk about his fear, this, in effect, takes the client's attention away from the fear-inducing object. The object now becomes the client's (secondary) construction of his fear. Now just as with any other act of perception, with fear as object, the client will have some affective tinge to that perception. That is, he will have feelings about having fear, but feeling about having fear are not the same thing as fear itself. A client can talk forever about the feeling that he has about being frightened without this necessarily having any impact upon the fear itself. Nor is it necessarily the case that eliminating the fear is the object of the therapeutic exercise. The fear might be or might once have been wholly appropriate. If what the client experiences in therapy is an exploration of secondary constructions and their concomitant feelings then he will learn to be more psychologically sophisticated and might pick up some doctrinal content from the therapist (for all therapists have theories about feelings), but will not necessarily learn to live more effectively. If, on the other hand, his time in therapy gives him a direct experience of enhanced aliveness through sharing his experience of encounters with significant others, sharpening his sense of their otherness, rehearsing alternative ways of responding to them, and appreciating them in new ways, then all of these experiences are likely to contribute directly to him having a more vibrant life.

If the range of response available to the therapist is limited by the therapy situation there is an obvious merit in the response staying as close as possible to the experiencing of the client. In the next sections we shall look at an approach that has been developed at the Amida centre[8] which attempts to do so. The caveats opened above apply to this methodology as much as to any other. Ultimately it is not the technique but the esteem that informs it that is therapeutically consequential, and so technique can be considered to be a medium rather than an agent. Nonetheless, a medium is needed and some mediums do function better or have less pitfalls than others.

Object-Centred Response

Self is a function of object responsiveness and it consists of a configuration of responses to the object world built up through experience, education, and strategy. It relies particularly upon the impressions of those times when such experiences have been more than normally vivid or challenging: the times when love or survival or both has been at stake. The person is not necessarily any longer conscious that what she is doing is utilising a response repertoire. She simply does what she does. She will feel, merely, that that is 'me', that that is how I am. The self psychologist will perhaps say that the person validates her self-concept by reference to her responses to objects and their responses to her, and that is true, but it is simpler to think that a person responds to objects and the way she learns to do so constitutes self.

From this perspective, when the untutored client comes and tells his story parading before the therapist verbal pictures of significant others, the other centred therapist will not say, "And how is this for you?" She will, rather, make an intervention along the lines of "Tell me more about this particular object." Thus if the client says, "My sister...." the therapist may say, "Tell me more about your sister. What is she like?" or, simply, "Your sister.....?" In other words, the therapist is interested in what the client is talking about and invites a deeper enquiry into those objects that are already naturally in the client's line of view. This type of response - the actual wording can obviously vary - is more natural, less technical, more in the flow of the client. It is less likely to arouse the client's suspicion and defensiveness. It is confirmatory for the client, demonstrating that the therapist is attentive and concerned about what the client is attentive to and concerned about. It is actually more client centred. Yet it is also third party centred and this is important. It demonstrates the therapist's loving regard for the client at the same time as inviting a more thorough going investigation of the client's regard for the other; for the third party that the client is concerned about. It will also be noted that this avoids any necessity for the therapist to ask the client, "What do you feel about your sister?" since as the client's perception of the sister becomes more vivid in the client's mind's eye how the client feels will be revealed directly to the therapist by being manifest in the client's manner in the room. The therapist will immediately see what response the perception of the sister conjures in the client. It will be live. The client's here and now experiencing will be vivid.

By inviting the client to bring the sister more sharply into focus the therapist also sharpens her own perception of her own image of the sister. As the client adds more details, the therapist's image of the sister will become better informed. Since all perceptions bring affective and cognitive over-tones, the therapist will now start to have subjective experiences related to the sister. Some of these will coincide with those of the client. Some may not. As therapist and client compare notes in this process new learning may emerge. This is essentially the process of empathy. Empathy for an other arises when one psychologically comes alongside that other and starts to see their world as they see it. One resonates to the other's pattern of esteem. While both are focussed on a third, this is as close as they get to each other's souls. One feels one's way, not so much into their self, as around their world. We wander together within it and examine its marvels.

Now, of course, the therapist may respond differently to the other than the client does. The client might say, "She has a shrill voice." Therapist and client have each known other persons with shrill voices in the past and the reaction that each has is likely to be coloured by their respective histories. The therapist thus experiences a double process, having both a natural-to-herself reaction and an empathic awareness of the client's reaction. This double experience inevitably colours the interaction between therapist and client and to some extent is the reason why the client does present this material. At some level the client wants to compare notes. Even if the therapist only makes accurate empathic responses, the client can tell from the voice tone the extent to which the therapist believes that the client's response to the other (in this case the sister) is inevitable or simply one of a number of possibilities. One of the things that therapy does is to bring supposed certainties into question. The therapist does not have to say, "Is that the only way to regard her?" in order to bring the matter into question. Nonetheless, the basic point here is that empathy arises through sharing an object in a process of object-regard. In that empathic process the manner of regard or esteem becomes apparent and may change. Consciously the therapist concerns herself with attentiveness to the objects that are important to the client and attempts to do so with the minimum of imposed evaluation. We can say, therefore, that the other centred therapist not only attempts to have unconditional positive regard for the client, but, more importantly, has such an unconditional regard for the client's others and relies upon the fact that the client's self, being a dependent variable, will change if esteem toward those others changes. This provides a route to therapy that does not have to directly confront the client's self structures or work through layers of character armour (Reich 1945/1972).

The therapist implicitly models esteem toward the client's

objects. This, of course, as in any therapy, does not work if done is a crass manner. It is definitely not, for instance, the therapist's duty to impose a positive evaluation upon the third parties that arise in the dialogue. It is likely that many of them will, at least initially, bear an at least partially negative value in the eyes of the client. The therapist's duty is to help the client to move toward truth and the truth may not always be clement or convenient. Perhaps the client will discover that her sister is even more of a villain than she initially suspected. Even in this scenario, however, the therapist is likely to hold the whole scenario within an encompassing positive attitude. The therapist's manner might in effect say, "Yes, the sister is a villain," but the therapist's sheer ability to be with the client in the 'presence' of this villain makes the tragedy bearable and yields stability of a higher order as we saw in our analysis of King Lear and theatrical tragedy in general. After all, what is the client really trying to do in this imaginary scenario? We may assume that it is troublesome to the client to have a villainous sister. This is difficult to cope with. It is difficult in the direct sense that the sister perhaps does things that harm the client. This direct harm is, however, unlikely to be the reason for bringing this matter to therapy, troublesome as it may be. It is, after all, a practical matter primarily. What is the nature of the psychological problem? Esteem theory suggests that fundamentally the problem is likely to be the frustration that the client experiences in not being able to have a satisfactory experience of loving her sister. One's siblings are presented by the existential situation of life as prime objects and therefore as ones that one shall love. However, siblings do not always act in ways that makes loving them a practical proposition. This is inherently frustrating at a deep level and is very likely to be the kind of problem that is brought to therapy. As in all cases, the basic problem is, "How do I love?"

Object-centred Enquiry

The therapist can help the client to explore the truth about the objects. The objects are likely to include such significant others as mother, father, siblings, spouse, work- or school-mates, lovers and anybody else who has been significant in the wider love life of the client. These are the people who have been the objects of the client's love and who have given the client the experience of disappointed love that has been instrumental in making him what he is. The experience of therapy allows the client to rework this material in two ways that have been long recognised by psychotherapy: through the material itself and through the resulting relationship with the therapist. We will come to the latter later. For the moment let us remain focussed upon the process of investigating the object(s).

The client presents difficulties in loving and the therapist invites a more searching investigation of the love objects. The client sifts through the evidence available about the object. The therapist facilitates this enquiry by encouraging the process while remaining as neutral as possible about its outcomes. Thus the therapist may say, "Tell me about Tom," "What's he like?" "Seeing him in your mind's eye at this moment, what is he doing?" "How is he looking at you?" "What might he be thinking?" "How did he come to that idea?" "What is important to him?" "What does he spend his time doing?" "Was he always like that?" "When did he change?" and so on. Remembering our basic caveat, this done simply as technique will not necessarily function well. It needs, as Rogers would say, to be congruent and backed with genuine esteem. However, if those conditions are met, this more than usually painstaking enquiry may go well. The client may have talked about the other in question many times but may have rarely met anybody who was genuinely interested. Why should they be? The significant other is only significant in this particular way for the client. There is no reason intrinsic to the self of anybody else why they should be interested. However, a second layer of meaning now opens up. When we press the question, 'Why should they be?' it is apparent that in natural life only the lover is really interested in the beloved's esteem for third parties. A concern for the client's objects is itself an expression of love and, in fact, if the therapist does not have a genuine esteem for the client then she is likely to find the work tedious and this will probably show. This is, therefore, a style of work that, while it gives the therapist an accurate reading of the client's core, also gives the client as good a reading of the therapist's authenticity.

In some approaches to therapy one is taught not to ask questions, but what seems to be important is to avoid asking questions that are not really questions. Many interventions that have the form of questions are really directions and are in the form of questions simply for reasons of courtesy. The kind of question that asks for relevant information that one genuinely does not know already and that one would really like to know, questions in which there is no element of subtle manipulation of the person to whom the question is addressed, are legitimate.

Thus therapist and client enter into an investigation of the third party. The client, through this process, may change his perception of the third party in some significant way. That change will bring about change in the client. Since self is a function of relation to objects, a change in relation to objects will directly induce a change in the self. It will do so without the therapist necessarily having made any direct investigation into the client's self nor put the client in the position of having to do so. Change may occur without the necessity of insight. Changed 'outsight' may be sufficient and even more powerful.

What sorts of things might commonly happen in this process? The client might discover that the object is more lovable than initially conceived. He might, for instance, arrive at the conviction "Although Dad did not love me in the way I wanted him to, he did love me in his own way." and this shift of perception may be sufficient to enable the client to love Dad again, at least at the level of finding respect. Such conviction is only likely to be full and convincing when the client is also convinced that he arrived at this conclusion himself and was not manipulated into it by the therapist. This is why the non-judgmental and unconditional attitude of the therapist is crucially important. Therapy is not achieved by the therapist persuading the client that such-and-such a person is not as bad as the client has painted them. It comes about when the client arrives at new conviction for himself. The therapist can support and encourage the process of enquiry, but must not attempt to tamper with the results of the client's experiment in truth.

This example alone is enough to demonstrate how a change in perception of a third party can transform the self in major ways. Believing that one is loved by one's parent, even a dead parent, is quite different from believing that one was hated or resented. No insight is required. Simply changing from one manner of esteem to the other effects a highly significant change in a person's mode of being in the world.

The above is not the only possible outcome. By entering into an investigation of significant others the client is finding out if he can cope with the truth or if he even dare face the truth. The therapist will be content if the client discovers that he can survive and continue to function even though the facts of life are adverse. Where a client has been particularly badly treated by those who should normally have been love objects for him, he will commonly have resorted to deception, including self-deception, as a means of coping. To put it in a more esteem theory way, we can say that in order to go on loving in life in any way at all he may screen out some of the information that reality is throwing at him. This screening out takes and wastes energy and yields various forms of dysfunction. The enterprise of therapy may sometimes, therefore, be that of experimenting with allowing in a larger quota of the awful truth while still finding ways to continue. This is a hazardous procedure. When the therapist begins to accompany the client on his exploration, the therapist does not know which kind of situation this is. If the therapist were unskilfully to try to influence the client to think better of the significant other when what is actually required is the attempt to allow in a fuller appreciation of the horrible facts, then the therapist will simply disqualify herself and make the therapy unworkable.

Nonetheless, if the other centred approach is correct, then the therapist also has to bear in mind that the client has to endure carrying an ineradicable urge still to love the other however bad the other has been. This is a second reason why persuasion is inappropriate. If there still is a way to love the other the client will find it and will do so by a means more skilful than any therapist is capable of advising. If the client does not do so it is because the way remains blocked and therapy must be loyal to the truth whatever it may be.

So at one extreme we have the scenario where a change of perception of the other leads to a renewal of love and at the other end we have that where the facts are sufficiently terrible to create an enduring barrier, at least for now. The client who emerges from uncertainty and ambivalence and arrives at the conviction, 'He really did always hate me and wish me dead and still does,' has actually made psychological progress. He might still find a way of respecting that person from a distance in a certain way, such as 'He had his reasons for being like that, poor man,' and/or he might have to cut off psychological contact, but even in the latter case will now do so in a cleaner and less energy wasting way and may have substantial areas of life where love is still possible. Such a development enables the client to move on.

Between these extremes we have two further typical kinds of case. In the first, the client arrives at a new more accurate perception of the other but this is not such as to make the other lovable in the old or originally desired way. In this case it may be that the client finds a new way of loving the person. Typically this, as in the more extreme case just mentioned above, involves the attainment of a higher degree of detachment. It is more loving to regard the other as an independent being. Doing so releases both parties. I will write more about this in the section on dimensions of loving below. In the second and by far the most common case, what emerges is a mixed picture. As the client enquires more and more closely into what they know and have experienced of the other, the other emerges as an increasingly complex being. Stereotyped ideas about them based upon one or two instances drawn from a lifetime of diverse experience start to crumble. The other starts to show through as a whole human being with strengths and weaknesses, achievements and failures, love, kindness, weakness and cruelty, all muddled up, as is the case with most people. As such a picture starts to emerge the therapist can trust the client to find the right course and the client is likely to experience an enrichment of life as the relationship to the other becomes more 'real'.

We can understand this readily from an esteem theory perspective. Life is messy. Somehow a person has to learn to love in the real world, which is the world where people are messy and the situations that they live in similarly. If the therapist remains even handed through an exploration of the client's life that reveals a series of real people with all the mixed characteristics that people typically have this provides ideal conditions in which the client can learn what he needs to learn in his own way.

The Pain of Love and Defending Against It

We have acknowledged that the path of love is difficult with many obstacles and have suggested that the way that each person tackles these is what is character forming. Character is frozen love. The unfortunate fact is that love can be painful. When we love we grieve. We grieve in major ways when the love object is completely lost, but we grieve in little ways day in day out since the love object is rarely if ever totally available.

If we consider personal love, "although personal love fulfils an otherwise unavoidable lack in our life, it opens us to radical pain and suffering and never fulfils the whole of its promise. Hence, while it promises the highest personal happiness and for many persons is an essential ingredient in genuine happiness, it often delivers us over to sorrow and disappointment for which it has no defence of comfort" (Ehman 1968, p.255). Although Ehman's theory of love is different from ours, seeing it as a way to try to make good shortfalls in the self, the perfection of which some regard as the aim of life, I can only concur with his observation of the normal course of events. Ehman does, however, come closer to the other centred position than many therapists in that although his approach is still self-based, he sees love and the reaching out to the beloved as core rather than incidental elements of what the self is. I do not think that we have to see love as a way of trying to make good deficiencies in the self. Rather it is the other way about. We desire to love and in the process a self of some sort comes into being to compensate for the defeats and deficiencies in our love. The process is, however, undeniably a hard one.

We are made by disappointment. Disappointment is painful and we have to find some way of handling it. In this way develop all the varied strategies that analytical psychology calls defences. The work of psychotherapy may be to try to achieve a degree of melting so that some of the frozen up love is made accessible once again. This, however, is a perilous passage since with the melting comes the revitalisation of the pain that caused the freezing in the first place. It may, therefore, not be sufficient to melt. It is also necessary to find new ways of coping with the pain of love when living in the fluid state.

Rogers, in his personal reflections, writes, "I want to move on to another area of my learning in interpersonal relationships - one that has been slow and painful for me. / I feel warmed and fulfilled when I can let in the fact, or permit myself to feel, that someone cares for, accepts, admires, or prizes me. Because of elements in my past history, I suppose, it has been very difficult for me to do this. For a long time I tended almost automatically to brush aside any positive feelings aimed in my direction. My reaction was, 'Who me? You couldn't possibly care for me. You might like what I have done, or my achievements, but not me.' This is one respect in which my own therapy helped me very much. I am not always able even now to let in such warm and loving feelings from others, but I find it very releasing when I can do so." (Rogers 1980, pp. 19-20). He goes on to recognise that some people flatter in order to obtain something, but acknowledges that love is sometimes genuine.

In this self-depiction Rogers talks in a personal way about how he had a habit of defending himself against the risks involved in loving. I am sure that everybody can recognise this even if the actual habits that they have individually developed differ in some respects from his. In a slightly more theoretical vein, Rogers writes elsewhere about defensiveness in the following terms.

"Defensiveness I have described in the past as being the organism's response to experiences which are perceived or anticipated as threatening, as incongruent with the individual's existing picture of himself, or of himself in relation to the world. These threatening experiences are temporarily rendered harmless by being distorted in awareness, or being denied to awareness. I quite literally cannot see, with accuracy, those experiences, feelings, reactions in myself which are significantly at variance with the picture of myself which I already possess. A large part of the process of therapy is the continuing discovery by the client that he is experiencing feelings and attitudes which heretofore he has not been able to be aware of, which he has not been able to 'own' as part of himself." (Rogers 1980, p.187).

Here Rogers comes very close to a description in line with the ideas of the unconscious and defence mechanisms postulated and found so useful by the analytic schools of psychotherapy.

An other centred approach can also accept the idea that we defend and that we develop characteristic ways of doing so and that these come to constitute character traits and also that, through therapy or life experience, some of these may be undone, redone, or modified. However, the other centred perspective would suggest that it is not the self-perception which is the primary thing being defended. Self-concept may indeed be, as it were, an intermediate factor, but what is really being defended against is surely the pain that can come with loving. When we love an other we make ourselves open to grief in various forms and we then defend against it. Those defences build character and personality. They shape the self and the self-concept comes along on the back of that. The self-concept represents an accumulation of such defences. The reason that one does not want to let that accumulation go is that it wards off pain. The pain is not, in origin, however, the pain of lost vanity, but the pain of lost love. Vanity is secondary.

Dimensions of Love

To love is to esteem the other. This applies whether the other is a person or anything else. One can love a cat, a garden, a work of art, a landscape. Some might find this odd philosophically, but it is not at all odd to the person in the street. Also, the person in the street will readily recognise that there are different degrees and kinds of love, though all share a common essential nature. We love some things and people 'with all our heart' whereas in other cases, love takes a more everyday or lower key form. A person may love her work in many degrees whether or not it frustrates her. The important point is to recognise that

117

frustration does not preclude love, it is an inevitable concomitant of love. The challenge of life is how to continue to love without the love being defeated by the disappointment and grief that inevitably comes with it. This can be clarified by distinguishing four dimensions of love as follows.

Recognising Lovability: Perceiving and discerning lovable features in the other

The most basic aspect of love is attraction. One perceives features of the other that one likes, admires, values and cherishes. This is esteem. Some features of the other may be immediately and easily lovable. Some only become lovable as we come to understand them. In an object, there may be simple basic characteristics like shape and colour that attract us. In a person, broadly speaking, we may repeat that what is most lovable is often that person's own capacity to love others, and this may have many expressions, showing in their boldness, their skill, their demeanour, their way of talking, a glance, a gesture and so on. We discern, as we think, the person's potential as much as their existing characteristics. Our perception of others is always interpreted (Spinelli 1989) because it is purposeful. We are assessing truth, but more vitally we look for love and lovability. In therapy the therapist demonstrates a kind of loving and the client recognises that capacity and finds it attractive. However, although attractiveness can be superficial, this is also a dimension with considerable depth. The superficial is not all that we find attractive and sometimes we are attracted in spite of superficial features that are unattractive. We are all familiar with the idea of the lovable rogue, as of the ugly duckling. It is an interesting fact that what is lovable is not coincident with what is good in every case or in all dimensions. We can sometimes recognise characteristics as lovable even when they are not superficially attractive. Esteem theory suggests that many of the 'twisted' characteristics of people are a result of their struggles to love in difficult circumstances and so are, as it were, frozen relics of love or of love's experience over the years. A person with a certain kind of discernment may be able to recognise this in a particular case and 'see the love in him' even when somebody else would fail to do so. Parallel considerations apply to the appreciation of non-obvious features in other love objects, including non-animate ones, and herein lies some of the mystery of art appreciation or differences of taste in regard to aspects of natural beauty.

Enduring Esteem: Carrying an attitude within oneself of positive esteem toward the other

It was tempting to put here as the second dimension of love something about the necessity for action: that love is not love unless it is acted upon and that would have been in keeping with a long line of empirical thought that has been persuasive in Western philosophy for several centuries. That way of thinking also has much to do with the increasingly exposed nature of modern life in which nothing counts unless it comes under public scrutiny, with the value that our society puts upon positive action, and also with the powerful status that science and empiricism has achieved in the public imagination, science being unable to recognise anything as existing that it cannot observe and measure. However, this is a modern outlook only and there is a long history of powerful literature that hinges upon the idea of undeclared love and, in this respect I am persuaded by the arguments of such thinkers as Iris Murdoch referred to above that the 'inner life' is also a consequential reality and that while it is the reality from which outward action commonly springs, and may have come into being upon the stimulus of experience of outward encounter, once established it exists independently of any such consequence or contingency. In other words, that it is false reasoning to say that a thought never really occurred if it never had any issue in action and a thought or feeling may persist without external reinforcement. This is also the common sense. Between lovers, what each is sensitive to is not so much what the other does as what indication that provides of how the other regards one. One might say 'I like it when you do that' or 'I don't like it when you....' but the question really in issue is 'Does she love me?' or 'Do I love her?' and one might well add 'really?' because appearances are often deceptive. Love involves a positive predisposition toward the other that is essentially 'inner' and persistent.

Truth & Mystery: Respect for the other as a being who, while independent of oneself in many ways, is, as oneself, subject to conditions beyond personal control

A third dimension of love seems to be provided by a realistic assessment of the fact that the other person, while substantially independent of oneself, is not independent of factors in the world over which he or she, as oneself, has limited if any control. These factors are both current and past. In other words, we might love the 'self' of the other, but that self is in thrall to a world.

Love has to accommodate the fact that the other may change for reasons that one could not predict or prevent. We are all dependent beings in a variety of ways. Love has to make allowances for the factors that bear upon the love object. The wife who castigates her husband for not being with her when the reason that he is not with her is a genuine requirement of a career that she urged him to enter, or the husband who takes no account of the fact that his wife does also have a career and is not therefore well placed to do all the household chores has in each case remained set in a stereotype of love or of social conduct and not fully entered into what it means to love a real human being in the real world.

Perhaps more significantly still, the other has a history that one knows only partially and is subject to many influences that are not explicable in terms of the factors of the immediate situation. Fullness of love is not the same as fullness of knowledge. Love accepts and esteems the mystery as well as the overt manifestation. To love somebody is not like a commercial contract where one has the opportunity to read all the small print. Rather it is the element of mystery that adds depth to love. Thus when two people get to know each other, as they assume, 'too well', the magic departs from the relationship. Thus it is counter-productive to try to be too rational in matters of love. Doing so destroys the very fabric of which love is made.

Much of the dishonesty that people engage in toward themselves and that occurs in supposedly love relationships has to do with the endeavour to eliminate the unknown. True love accepts that the human consciousness as well as the human existential situation in the world has an ever-open frontier. It is loving to listen to the other in a way that facilitates enquiry beyond the already known, yet without any expectation of, as it were, emptying the ocean. Furthermore, one of the things that remains eternally unfathomable about the other is his love itself. We never directly perceive the other's love. We divine it from its effects. In itself it remains ever ineffable.

Otherness: Recognising that the other is indeed other

Love is love of what is other. When we do not recognise the otherness of the object then love is inevitably compromised, yet we rarely recognise it fully. Many people conceive love as a kind of unity or merger, but this idea is not really helpful. It is less than fully loving to regard the other person as part of oneself. Despite the common expression in which a marital partner refers to their spouse as their 'other half', love requires a basic separation. To love is to esteem the other as an other and to allow them to be other. "The more the separateness and differentness of other people is realized, and the fact seen that another man has needs and wishes as demanding as one's own, the harder it becomes to treat that person as a thing." (Murdoch 1970, p.64). This consideration is highly relevant to therapy. Often enough what obstructs the client's ability to love the significant other in question is a form of clinging that masquerades as love but is actually a form of anxious possessiveness. I have put this dimension last because, perhaps strangely, it seems to represent the highest development of love. The highest love is non-possessive love in which the lover only wants what is best for the other. This is what the Greeks called *agape* and some theologians will say that only God is fully capable of such love (Nygren 1939). Our love for one another is inevitably eros whereas God's love for us is agape. Nonetheless, even in human love, the dimension of seeing the other *as an other* is important and is a crucially important indicator of maturity.

In taking this approach I am aware of going against a wide range of opinion.

"Many people who have written about love or have thought about their love experiences have discerned that one major problem that threatens both the happiness of love and its very existence is the conflict between the desire for an intimate psychological union and the contrary need to maintain an independent identity... we desire to join our life with the life of another person, to mingle or merge ourself with the self of the other... at the same time, a secure sense of ourself as a distinct individual depends on maintaining more than a semblance of separateness." (Soble 1989, p.1)

However, I wish to challenge the notion of love as 'mingling and merging' and an alternative to identity and selfhood. Selfhood need not be seen as the goal of life, but a means. We create a self in order to be lovable and we create it out of our essays in love. This does not mean that love consumes us, it doesn't. Love involves fully respecting what is other and therefore different, mysterious. When people think about love they tend to focus in upon one relationship, paradigmatically, either marriage or the parent-child bond. However neither of these reaches its high-point in merger and they are not the only loves in a life. Such relationships generally fall into a state approximating merger through fear of the wider world. A person can be very lonely within a merged marriage. They might cling to it desperately fearing something worse, but the person who has an outgoing attitude that encompasses many interests, who esteems many aspects of her world, is a more consummate lover. This does not mean that she has many love affairs; she might be a faithful spouse; but her attitude to life is appreciative and she feels that she is enriched by many things. The idea that love is enhanced by being concentrated on one object is false. It may be right to concentrate one's conjugal love on one person, but if one does not rejoice in the bounty of life all around one will not have much to offer to that relationship. Further, one will be inclined to cling in a manner that actually impedes the love even of that central bond in one's life and so one may inadvertently spoil it.

These four dimensions help us, I hope, to discern the working of love. They are certainly not comprehensive in the sense of being the only things that one could say about this inherently limitless subject. However, these four do describe major features of what it means to love that are not always immediately obvious. A great many of the cases that come before a psychotherapist involve failure in one of these four domains.

Further, while I do primarily have love between human beings in mind, all four dimensions do apply to other forms of love. If a person loves a painting by Picasso, that love must include these elements. She must see the painting as an object, as something that is independent of herself. Between herself and the picture there will be a relationship. The painting is something in her life, but not something that she can voluntarily shape and determine. It has already been made and its content is not subject to her will. It has impact. It is, to use an existentialist term, gegenwelt, (Brazier 1991) something that stands over against herself and consequently puts her self into relief and into question. She appreciates that the painting is subject to real world exigencies and factors (including factors in the mind of Picasso) that she has no control over. Simplistically this means that the painting is not available to her just when and where she wants it. More profoundly and importantly it means that the painting will always have an element of mystery. She will never fully understand it. Even if she studies art in depth and knows the whole history of how Picasso came to paint the picture and everything he has ever said about it and she has had the picture on her wall for twenty years, it will still be a mystery. That sense of mystery will add depth to what she does find lovable about the picture. There will be aspects that appeal to her directly, such as the colours, the design, the whole voice of the picture. These things together ensure that the picture speaks to her and that she carries the picture within her subjective life tinged with a positive halo. This does not mean that she never experiences any negative feelings toward it. If it did not also resist her she would not love it as it would not engage her. She might sometimes think, "I wish I had never seen that picture," but it remains. It becomes part of her. Her self is coloured by it.

What I am suggesting, therefore, is that although we are educated to divide the world into human and non-human domains (sometimes admitting our pets or other animals onto the human side of the line), this division is something that we have learnt and is not part of our fundamental nature. The division that is fundamental is between what we love (in whatever degree) and what we do not. The category of things that we do not love become resources that we use in our loving, but they are not, to us, objects worthy in themselves. When Martin Buber distinguishes between the I-Thou and the I-it relationship (Buber 1970), he is saying something similar. Of course, it is possible for things to cross from one side of this divide to the other. Perhaps when we go into a shop we tend to treat the person behind the counter as an 'it', but in another circumstance, or when we have more time to stop and chat, we start to see them as 'thou'. I am not sure, but I suspect that in Buber's philosophy it is quite difficult for anything to be a 'thou' that is not at least human, whereas I suspect that in our basic nature we inhabit a universe that is, to our primitive mind, animistic. Everything is capable of having a soul (anima) and soul is what is loved. In this sense the 'primitive' person who can talk to rocks and sense the rock's soul lives in a world that is more fully a universe of love than the sophisticated person who has pared down the domain of ensouled life to a minimum and correspondingly exploits much and loves very little.

Dimensions of Love Lacking as Diagnostic Categories

The four dimensions of love set out above are a useful way of thinking about many of the problems that come before a psychotherapist. If our basic need is to love and esteem our world of others, then it is along one or other of these dimensions, or several of them, that things can go wrong.

Enmeshment

The problem of love being impeded by an inability to see the other as really being an other is common. Thus, we may regard our parents with a kind of love, but not actually conceive of them as separate beings with lives of their own, and reasons of their own for what they do. We tend to have exaggerated 'fantasies of reference', by which I mean that we interpret everything that they do in reference to ourselves. If they are late for a meeting it is not because the bus did not come, but because they no longer love one. We act as though we imagine that their life only functions in relation to ourselves and, correspondingly, we feel that we are part of them and act as though they are responsible for what we do. This kind of merged thinking leads to a loss of respect and of responsibility. Similar things can happen in any love relationship. Such phenomena are common between spouses. A spouse can harbour resentment for not having been able to do something, feeling that the other had not given permission for it, when, in fact, the other was completely unaware of the issue. The tendency to assume that the other can read one's mind or that they are responsible for whatever one does is common. The work of therapy may sometimes be to help a person disentangle themselves from the other, or, more correctly, disentangle the other from their own self. Until they do they cannot see the other as a being in their own right and love remains compromised.

A person may mistake this merged condition for love and many theories of human development assume that the infant begins life in a condition of psychological merger with mother and only gradually extricates from it. However, it may be that it is actually the parent who sees the child as part of self and the child that later has to fight for independence. The seeming miracle of having produced new life from out of one's own body is difficult to adjust to. Also, love only fully blossoms when it has enough room to be genuine. A mother might have a baby 'in order to have somebody to love me'. Now, the child will naturally love the mother, but if the child feels under an unrelenting obligation to love the mother this will actually create a barrier to the child doing so satisfactorily. It is like the situation where one is learning to drive in a dual control car with an instructor who never lets you actually take control. You do not learn. The impulse to love one's most significant others, of whom mother stands first in the list, is no doubt in-built, but loving involves learning. There are innumerable things that I have to learn about love as my life unfolds. If the mother is too anxious the child's learning is impeded.

This sort of problem is very common. The client comes to the psychotherapist and tells her story. As she tells it she describes the various significant others in her life. The manner in which she does so informs the therapist whether or not she regards those others as independent beings or as enmeshed. The enmeshment may be that she feels part of them or that they are part of her or both. It is likely to show up in ideas about responsibility and the feelings that come therewith, such as resentment, feeling trapped, outrage when the other acts independently, guilt when one thinks independently, a sense of invisible barriers that must not be crossed and so on.

Disrespect

We tend to assume that we know the people we love. Not uncommonly, a spouse acts as though he knows his wife better than she knows herself or vice versa. Love is impeded by too great an assumption of knowledge about the other. There has to be some space and freedom in the relationship for love to blossom. Of course, this means containing a degree of anxiety. Love often entails commitment, but humans are fully aware that commitment can be broken. This has become a more serious risk in the modern world where people no longer live in small tight knit communities, but in large, rambling social networks where the quotient of commitment is often extremely low and anonymity a possibility. Modern surveys that ask people how many others they fully trust or would confide in often show results with an average lower than one. In modern life we doubt that anybody will stand by us through thick and thin and so the urge to try to control can sometimes become very strong.

In the past control was substantially done for us by the social structure. Thus parents may assume that their child will be their creation. They feel responsible for what the child does and what becomes of him. To a degree this is not unreasonable. However, research suggests that parents are actually by no means as influential as is commonly assumed (Harris 1998) and, in any case, it is not in the nature of love to regard the other as one's puppet or creation.

Love is a respect for the living principle in the other and life is not reducible to a mechanism. The parent that loves the child, therefore, has to regard the child with awe and respect the mystery. One may have, through the sexual act, made this child, but the child is a new being and the loving parent marvels at what has come into the family's midst. The child may prove to have the makings of a fine upright citizen or may be destined to be a failure or a villain. The parent does not know. The parents' duty is to do their best for the child and in their love they will support the child through what then develops and befalls, but the child has to live his or her life and loving parents make that more readily possible. They cannot mould the child as one might clay, but they can equip him or her with skills, manners and resources and, above all, they can love him or her which will help to ensure confidence.

Dishonesty, Resentment and Bitterness

Love involves an enduring basic feeling of esteem for the other. It is rare, however, for this feeling to be completely unconditional. We want to be reinforced by information that comes back from the other that our love is received and received in a manner that fits with our own intention and concept. However, the other person does not necessarily see things the way we do. Love relationships are very commonly poisoned by elements of bitterness.

They are also eroded by anxiety. This may be related to fears about self-evaluation. In a relationship of person A and person B, let us say, B loves A and wants evidence, as did King Lear, that A loves B in return. B realises that A's love is related to the esteem that A has for B. B can then easily become obsessed with trying to read indications of A's esteem from every remark or act of A. This can lead either to bad feeling and bitterness or to dishonesty as each partner tries to avoid the arising of the uncomfortable situation. There are many variant scenarios. Broadly, we can say that a strong concern about whether one is loved tends to be quite destructive of love relationships. Just as one can only ride a bicycle by sailing forward and if one starts to examine what one is doing one is likely to fall off, so, in a relationship, too much introspection into the process can cause capsize.

Inability to Perceive What is Lovable in the Other

Most basically, love is impeded by blindness to the positive qualities of the love object. Relationships can become stale. The partners can stop seeing each other. Love involves seeing and listening. However, if seeing and listening to the other become unsatisfying then love will be hindered. Like all the other pitfalls touched on in this section, this is a two way street. Marital partners may have stopped listening to one another, either in that they no longer spend time hearing the other or in that when the other speaks they have already prejudged what might be said. Part of this development is likely to be that they have found what the other says has ceased to be interesting. This, in turn, may be a function of the fact that nothing new occurs, which may, in turn be a result of the partners living overly mutually enmeshed lives. Each life is a kind of art object that is continually remade. It draws attention in part through its renewal. However, the degree to which an object holds esteem is also a function of the maintenance of 'aesthetic distance' and we shall now, therefore, examine the significance of this factor.

Part Five:

Issues of Transference and Technique

Aesthetic Distance and Oestrostasis

The effectiveness of both art and therapy is related to aesthetic distance. The person who is over-distanced from an object, be that object a piece of art, a significant other person in his life, his work, or whatever, is bored. A person who is under-distanced is troubled. In neither case can the object function fully as a love object, love is consequently frustrated and one experiences disappointment. Persons who are in either an under-distanced or an over-distanced state in regard to matters of importance are 'blocked', hindered in their full participation in life. It is as though energy does not flow and the person's ability to engage, love, work and learn is impeded. If such a condition persists overly then, as we earlier noted that Freud remarked, one is bound to become sick.

The matter of aesthetic distance is well expounded by Thomas Scheff in his book *Catharsis in Healing Ritual and Drama* (Scheff 1979/2001). "In dramatic criticism, a drama is considered to be underdistanced if it evokes raw emotion in audiences to the point that its members become so drawn into the dramatic action that they forget where they are; they react as if they were participants in, rather than observers of, the drama. Such experiences increase rather than decrease, tension levels in the audience. In overdistanced drama, the audience is unmoved. Members of the audience are entirely observers of the dramatic action, with no participation at all. / At aesthetic distance, the members of the audience become emotionally involved in the drama, but not to the point where they forget that they are also observers. Aesthetic distance may be defined as the simultaneous and equal experience of being both participant and observer" (p.57).

Some people experience life in an under-distanced way much of the time. This is part of the problem of the schizophrenic. Some people are habitually over-distanced, as, stereotypically, the jaded sophisticate, but over-distancing in some degree is probably the common lot of modern mankind.

Exposure to strong or shocking stimuli lead most people to adjust their distancing. This is why people become jaded with violent films or pornography and this then may generalise making their life seem dull. The person who has lived in high-stimulus situations may find ordinary life over-distanced, as, for instance, the soldier returning from war. People who have been abused may sometimes unconsciously seek situations where the abuse may be repeated because, having adjusted their set, the seeming dullness of ordinary life is difficult to bear. I have heard similar reports from recovering schizophrenics. Being mad was terrible, but it was never dull.

In therapy, the therapist and client together, as it were, become audience to the drama of the client's mitwelt (private world).[9] For this to be a meaningful experience, aesthetic distance is required. The therapist can assist in achieving this. Depending upon the manner of the therapist's response to the client's disclosures, distance will shorten or lengthen. Broadly, distance may be reduced by (a) vividness and closeness of imagery, (b) immediacy of language, (c) emotionality, (d) speech in the present tense, (e) specificity of detail; and it may be extended by (a) imagining imagery further away, (b) abstract language, (c) intellectuality, (d) description in the past tense or in no particular time frame, (e) generality.

People adjust distance in response to stimuli in order to maintain a habitual 'oestrostasis' (level of stimulation). Different people have different habitual levels depending upon habituation. If a person's oestrostat is set low, then small matters may excite them strongly whereas if it is set high they may have difficulty avoiding boredom. In any case, we all adjust to immediate circumstances in an attempt to approximate to what we are used to, but since personal setting varies, some people will find others boring or over-stimulating as the case may be.

Aside from this day-to-day adjustment, a person's long-term setting is a function of past experience. Trauma has the effect of leaving the person afraid of over-stimulation. This leads them both to reduce their engagement with ordinary life and under-function and also to have episodes, often in dreams, when they become again under-distanced and re-traumatize. Therapy, like art, depends upon sustaining attention at the optimum distance level so that the oestrostat can be reset, as it were.

Art objects aim to achieve an optimum aesthetic distance so that the attention is held without the critical faculty being paralysed. Religious ritual achieves an optimum distance when, in the course of the rite, belief and disbelief are held in perfect balance, the participant both believing, say, that they are conversing with the god and, at the same time, that they are simply a group of people following a liturgical script. Therapy aims to maintain optimum distance by keeping the client in relation to significant others in a fully engaging manner that is neither abstract nor over-whelming.[10] In this way, art, ritual and therapy all have the purpose of restoring or enhancing the status of the other as a love object.

A Protocol for Object Related Therapy

We should now be in a position to set out in a fairly precise manner the basic theory and method of object related therapy as one species of other centred therapy, an approach to working with the client in an other centred way in which the methodology is consistent with esteem theory. It is not suggested that this is the only possible way of working in an other centred way. Rather, our contention is that all therapy actually works, insofar as it does, because of the effectiveness of its other centric components. In this section, however, let us confine ourselves to clarifying what an object related method of work looks like.

Where:

1. Functional Boundaries:
   A therapist works consistently within a bounded frame appropriate to the ambient culture, the function of the agency, and the contract individually agreed, either explicitly or implicitly, with the client; and

2. Esteem:
   Within those functional bounds, the therapist has a sustained unconditional positive regard for and confidence in the client and the client's process, regarding the client as inherently loveable; and

3. Respect:
   Gives evidence of treating the client as a responsible other, a distinct character worthy of respect, subject to the vicissitudes of conditions in the environment, attempting to live a constructive life as best can; and

4. Discernment of Significant Objects:
   The therapist elicits, discerns and takes genuine interest in those objects presented by the client that have a power and influence upon the client's perception; and

5. Maintenance of Optimum Distance:
   The therapist speaks and acts in a way that enables the client to maintain an optimum aesthetic distance from significant objects, exploring their reality; and

6. Non-condemnatory AttitudeThe therapist does not exhibit any degree of condemnation of either the client or the client's significant objects;

then it may be expected that the client will, in constructive or problem resolving ways, change his or her mode of relating to others, not limited only to the objects considered, but generalising to other aspects of life also.

In order to carry out such work the therapist needs to establish the kind of empathic regard in which the therapist experiences regarding the client's significant objects from the standpoint of the client as if she were the client without losing consciousness of this being 'as if' (i.e. has empathic regard without falling into identification).

In the course of the work the client may experience changes that are not ends in themselves, but rather epiphenomena of therapeutic change taking place. These may include changes in a constructive or resolving direction in regard for the significant objects themselves, in attitude toward, feeling about and construction of the client's mitwelt (experienced frame of reference), or in self-concept. In the course of therapy the client may report such changes and the therapist may acknowledge them by way of accompanying communication.

The term 'accompanying communication' refers to communication by the therapist necessary for the maintenance of a proper working environment and relationship with the client and of the tempo of the session. The protocol does not preclude the therapist from engaging in normal social pleasantries or commenting on transient changes in the client's demeanor, so long as these do not interfere with the task of helping the client bring significant objects into focus in an optimally distanced manner.

When the client fails to do so, as when the client is silent or wholly focussed upon abstractions, the therapist maintains a warm actively empathic stance.

Thus, object related therapy prescribes that the therapist concern herself with the significant objects naturally presented by the client in a manner that intensifies the client's examination of those objects and leads him to reconsider the evidence known to him about them until some shift, positive or negative, occurs in his perception of them, and to do this within a context of unconditional positive regard for the client in his relation to those objects.

This description provides us with a formal account of the object related method. Now a particular aspect of this approach that still needs specific attention is the case where the significant object that the client is under the spell of is the therapist herself. This is the matter that in other approaches is called 'transference'.

Transference: The Therapist as Object

The Idea of Transference

In psychotherapy the client meets a therapist. The therapist is bound to become a significant object for the client in some degree. A useful rule of thumb classification of psychotherapy and counselling cases is to divide them into those where the client continues to regard the therapist as a resource, a thing, part of an I-it relationship, and those where the therapist has in some way become important to the client beyond mere service provision. The former cases exist in the simplest instances of counselling as advice giving and this utilitarian attitude may persist even in some cases of simple psychotherapy where the client remains strongly focussed upon his own world and its issues. Nonetheless, in the majority of cases, the therapist does become a figure of significance to the client to a degree greater than is required by his function as a service provider. This means that it becomes consequential with what kind of esteem the client regards the therapist.

Thus there are two kinds of material or data in psychotherapy. Firstly there is the mitwelt, the data that the client has about his world outside the therapy. The client, as it were, brings his mitwelt with him. On entering therapy, however, he encounters a new 'world', that of the therapy relationship, and in this the person of the therapist is of great importance. Freud pointed out that there will be a powerful tendency for the client to construe the therapy situation using habits of thought and perception already established in the context of his earlier life. Freud came to regard this circumstance as one of great utility. He spoke of 'transference' meaning the transfer into the therapy interaction of ways of relating that have their roots in the client's past life, especially, Freud thought, in relations with primary parental figures. Thus the client was likely to treat the therapist the way that the client had learnt to treat the parent. If, for instance, the parent had been authoritarian, then the client will assume that the therapist is authoritarian even if the therapist is not actually acting in an authoritarian manner. We can readily see that this means that if the therapist can discern how it is that the client is regarding him, especially in those instances when that regard seems to be out of kilter with the real flow of events in the therapy room, then such discernment may enable the therapist to draw conclusions about the way that the client regarded primary figures in his life. To put this differently, the type of esteem that the client manifests toward the therapist is likely to be the type of esteem that he has in other important areas of his life, and, depending upon the view that one holds about personality development, this may also yield conclusions about how the client came to have such a regard.

The term transference has come to have a variety of specialist meanings within psychoanalysis, but the general idea is not exceptional. We all tend to construe new situations in the light of those with which we are familiar and especially those that have made a formative impression upon us. Nonetheless, the idea of transference did create considerable controversy amongst the followers of Rogers. Rogers thought that the condition of congruence that he suggested as necessary for successful psychotherapy would have the effect of minimising the occurrence of transference. If the therapist is congruent (i.e. 'being herself') then there will be plenty of evidence within the therapy relationship about what the therapist is 'really' like and correspondingly less scope for the client to develop fantasies about the therapist. Client-centred therapists were, therefore, likely to stress the 'real' reactions that clients realistically had to the therapist such as resentment if the therapist seemed condescending or "loving feelings may arise in the client from an unexpected and very welcome depth of understanding on the part of the therapist.... [several other examples of helpful behaviour are given]" (Rogers 1986, in CRR p.129). Rogers recognised a "second category of client reactions" that:

> "are emotions that have little or no relationship to the therapist's behavior. These are truly 'transferred' from their real origin to the therapist. They are projections. They may be triggered by something in the therapist - 'You look like my father,' or 'You resemble a man I despise' - but the intensity of the feeling comes from within the client, and is not due to the behavior of the therapist. These projected feelings may [include] love, sexual desire, adoration [or] hatred, contempt, fear, mistrust. Their true object may be a parent or other significant person in the client's life. Or, ... negative attitudes toward the self, which the client cannot bear to face. From the client-centred point of view, it is not necessary... to determine whether they are therapist caused or are projections... all these attitudes... are best dealt with in the same way. If the therapist is sensitively understanding and genuinely acceptant and non-judgmental, therapy will move forward through these feelings. There is absolutely no need to make a special case of attitudes that are transferred" (*ibid.*).

It seems that Rogers thought (perhaps, wrongly) that it is an aim of psychoanalytic therapies to generate transference and consequent dependency. In fact, in analytic therapy transference is more commonly regarded as an obstacle to the therapeutic alliance, but it is seen as one that can yield important data for analysis. Since Rogers did not see himself as engaged in analysis, but in facilitating a process of enabling the 'self-actualising tendency' to fulfil its purpose, he saw no particular utility in transference phenomena, though it seems clear from the above that he recognised their existence in theory.

The Transference Controversy in the Person-Centred Approach

Nonetheless, the issue of transference did become a matter of hot controversy in the person centred movement fuelled, no doubt, by professional rivalries between therapists of the person-centred and analytical schools. In 1984, Shlien published a paper called "A Counter-theory of Transference" (Levant & Shlien 1984, pp. 153-181) in which he made the provocative remark

"'Transference' is a fiction, invented and maintained by therapists to protect themselves from the consequences of their own behavior."

Shlien looks at the origin of the term transference historically, showing how Freud invented the term at least in part in response to the case of 'Anna O', an analysand of his colleague Breuer, who developed love feelings toward Breuer that caused Breuer considerable family embarrassment. On the basis of Breuer's Anna O case Freud developed his 'cathartic' or 'abreactive' method, which he then used with a series of clients of his own with some success. Freud later gave up this method, substituting the method of analysis of unconscious contents, especially analysis of the transference. Shlien is critical of Freud's idea of transference as a 'neurosis'. Part of Shlien's point is that if one enters into a relationship with another person in which one listens to their secrets and troubles and does so in a caring and compassionate way such as they have rarely previously experienced, it is not really surprising if the client falls in love with you and to interpret them doing so as a form of pathology is a betrayal and disservice.

Shlien's article was reprinted in 1987 in the Person-Centered Review (Shlien 1987) and the whole of the following issue of the periodical was devoted to responses from Ernst Beier, Constance Fischer, Harold Greenwald, Arnold Lazarus, Salvatore Maddi, Julius Seeman, Hans Strupp, and Carl Rogers himself. However, Rogers himself died on 4 February 1987 and the next issue of the Review was dedicated to tributes in memory of him. Nonetheless, the controversy over transference continued into the subsequent November issue. Opinions were divided. This whole debate is well worth reading and thinking through, not least Shlien's own response to those who criticise his view (Shlien 1987b). He holds to his view that to hold to the idea of transference is a defence for the therapist and unproductive therapeutically, muddling the understanding that the therapist and client may arrive at which is what he believes to be therapeutic. I recommend all this as well worthy of study and hope that therapists studying this matter will acquaint themselves with this important material.

My main purpose here is to see how the matter looks from an other centred perspective. Let us start by recapitulating some basic points of theory. The growing person is driven to fulfil their need to love the significant others in their life. Doing so always meets with obstacles. There is frustration and disappointment due to the nature of life, the child's lack of omnipotence, failures of understanding, failures of love on the part of the significant others, and so on. The growing person grows psychologically by finding ways to surmount these difficulties. The ways that they find to do so have consequences both for their psyche and for the circumstantial frame in which their life develops. All this builds character. We might think of the character in question as polished or as twisted, but it is what it is and it springs from this same drive. Thus, just as Rogers saw the potato plants in the cellar struggling toward the light and concluded that there is one basic dive, so in esteem theory we see all the different manifestations of character as deriving from the love drive, struggling through more or less clement conditions, like trees that may grow in a fertile valley or on a windswept hillside. The latter may be twisted, but that is their character, and that too is lovable, in its own way.

Character includes mastery of a variety of strategies that give flexibility in oestrosatsis so that a person can expand their appreciation to a wider range of love objects from the most significant to the most trivial without the love drive becoming unduly blocked, frustrated or defeated.

From this perspective, there is a sense in which Shlien and the advocates of transference theory are both right. The client brings his character into the therapy encounter. It does bear all the traces of past experience. He is inclined to read the therapist in ways that may be surprising to the latter and may, in a sense, not be realistic in terms of the here and now situation as it might be seen by an unbiased researcher, yet, all that Shlien says is also still true: it is not really that surprising if the client responds to the therapist's loving attention by developing affective bonds. I was discussing recently with a group of students and we came to the subject of whether Western therapy methods had application in non-Western countries and I told them how I had been to some countries where it would be completely unacceptable to say the sorts of things that Western people say to their therapists to somebody that one was not related to by close social or kinship bonds. In some cultures, if you have shared such secrets, the implication is that you are now related in a way that creates bonds and obligations, such as that you should be willing to go out and fight and die for one another. Most Western therapists do not see such entrained obligations as part of the therapy contract. Nonetheless, therapy is concerned with intimate matters and even in our society intimacy has natural implications of enduring relationship. Some of these natural implications have been undermined by the conventions of modern life, but that does not erase them from our instinctive make-up.

Transference as a Transition to (Re-)Loving

It seems, therefore, that transference may be a useful theoretical idea, but for other centred theory the phenomena that transference relates to are going to be understood in a slightly different way. The client's character shows the marks of his life experience, just as a gnarled piece of wood shows its grain. The therapist attempts to understand. If the therapist discerns the genetic dimension of a particular aspect of character that is interesting. Such understanding may, but does not necessarily, help the therapist to be more understanding. It is not, however, the understanding of information that is therapeutic, it is the act of understanding appearing as a species of love. Whether the client is healed or not is a function of whether and to what extent the client's own capacity to love can flow and whether it can find channels to do so that will continue to function in the life situation that the client now inhabits. It might seem a temporary solution to the client's blocked love drive if the client starts to love the therapist. However, the therapist cannot marry her clients. The fact that the client is experiencing some flow of loving feelings might be a step in the right direction, but if that love flows only toward the therapist this does not represent a viable long term solution and if the therapist were to become involved with the client in a relationship which broke the boundaries of the therapeutic contract then the therapy would become unworkable and a betrayal would occur. At most, therefore, the love feelings that a client might develop for a therapist can be a transitional phenomenon. Further, it must, since therapy is time limited, involve disappointment.

The therapist would prefer to be a catalyst to the client

finding other love objects. This transition may be a very difficult and taxing circumstance for the therapist, but faith must be maintained that the client will get beyond it and will in due course find other more suitable objects in which to invest their now more available feelings. This is not by any means the only sequence that a course of therapy may follow, but it is sometimes what happens. Now in this circumstance, an analytical therapist will see her duty as to analyse the transference and a person-centred therapist will see it as to remain congruent and empathic. From an other centred point of view it probably does not matter whether the client and therapist discuss the possible history of the client's feeling or not. What is effective is the fact that the client is relearning how to love and, hopefully, eventually, how to do so appropriately.

It does matter, however, whether the client can arrive at aesthetic distance in his perception of the therapist. If the attachment that the client feels for the therapist is so strong that it disturbs the client's functioning in life and ability to turn their attention to other significant objects then we have an under-distanced situation and this is disruptive to the therapy. Equally if the client fails to engage with the therapist as a significant force in his life then the therapy will lack weight or effectiveness. Rogers believed that this capsize can generally be avoided by the therapist being 'real', but this is not a totally convincing proposition. Literature, and one thinks immediately of Midsummer Night's Dream, is full of accounts of inappropriate obsessional love that is not averted by the love object being 'real'. The difficulty involved in arriving at the position of aesthetic distance within the therapeutic relationship can be substantial in any approach to therapy and its achievement is one of the indicators of success. Therapy is set up to be a 'take it and leave it' situation. The juxtaposition of esteem and functional boundaries predispose the client to both invest and detach all at once. The therapist must sometimes make one or other of these factors more salient in the interests of retaining optimum distance in the therapeutic alliance. However, in the general run of therapy, optimum distance is approximated naturally through the client and therapist working together and the therapist maintaining an empathic regard for the client's objects within the 'as if' condition. In other words, while client and therapist are both interested in things that are interesting and important to the client, and the therapist's regard for those objects approximates that of the client, the therapist and client will automatically and unconsciously maintain a good workable distance.

In the ideal case, the person of the therapist is a catalytic object. Stereotypically, a client who has difficulty loving comes into therapy and at the end of successful therapy they now are able to love in a manner appropriate to their circumstances in life. Along the path from the first point to the second the client will have had feelings about the therapist. These might have been intense or mild. They may have included affection, hatred, desire, and disappointment - a great range. All these feelings are related to love and in a sense they reflect the client's love history in life. By the end of therapy, the client needs to have reached a position where he is invested in love relations outside of therapy to a degree sufficient to make the therapy no longer necessary. Through therapy, the loving nature or the origins in love of the client's actions may become more apparent and the client may find or change love objects. The aim of the whole procedure, however, is that the client find new, more viable, ways to love.

Building Character

There is another aspect of this same issue and material, however. One of the reasons that Freud gave up the cathartic method was that he came to believe that its results were not all that he originally thought. However, this judgement on his part has been interestingly critiqued by Scheff who points out that Anna O, whose real name was Bertha Pappenheim, "became the first social worker in Germany, one of the first in the world... founded a periodical and several institutes" (Scheff 1979/2001, pp.41-42) as well as working for women's emancipation and child welfare. By modern standards she was a great success, but Freud seems to have counted her a failure because she never married nor had children.

It is tempting to say that the case was one of successful sublimation; more successful, in fact, than that achieved by many people in Freud's time. Bertha became a strong character to a degree that gave her a progressive, if not revolutionary, impact in the society of her day. She, in a significant way, helped to change the world. Six or seven decades later, I myself and thousands of others were to train in the profession that she helped to establish and by that time the position of women had changed substantially. Scheff asks whether Freud was right to give up the cathartic method. The interest in this same material here is that, if, as Scheff suggests, the Anna O case was actually more successful than Freud judged to be the case, then it is an example of the creation of a remarkable character through love and its disappointment.

Among Freud's many followers was Otto Rank. Unlike Freud who tended to work with members of conventional bourgeois families, Rank's patients included many artists and 'eccentric' personalities. A person much influenced by Rank was Jessie Taft, who, like Pappenhiem, became a pioneering social worker, in this case in Philadelphia. She was a to be a substantial influence upon Rogers. Rogers took from her the idea, common to a number of therapeutic approaches, that the boundaries set by the therapist increased the intensity of the therapeutic encounter. Thus, although Rogers espoused non-directivity, it was still generally the therapist who decided how long a therapeutic session would be and who set a fee, though some of Rogers' followers thought that these areas too should be in the domain of client self-determination.

Taft, however, saw the 'boundary issues' as crucial. She saw therapy as "a process in which the individual learns to utilize the therapeutic hour without undue fear, resistance, resentment or greediness, learns to take it and also leave it without denying its value and without trying to keep it forever because of its value" (quoted in Raskin 2005, p.19). Raskin adds, "Rogers advocated other limits in the interest of enhancing therapy." We can see that for Taft, the shift in the client's attitude toward the therapy itself and in particular toward its time-limited nature was itself a major indicator of advance in maturity.

Thus, in esteem theory terms, we have said that life is a process in which love is the strong force, yet it is endlessly frustrated. Therapy provides a time when that love may be demonstrated, re-found and exercised, yet within limits. The client cannot have all that he wants of the therapist. This is a frustrating situation. Life is like that: the cake is delicious, but only small portions are served. It is the working together of this supply and limitation that can generate optimum distance. It would seem that the optimum distance that is character building involves both the experience of love and of its disappointment and that this can, and ideally does, lead to a sublimation and development of capacity to love that extends not just to significant human others but to good in all its altruistic forms.

Therapy replicates the general situation of love evoked and frustrated, yet does so in a more conscious way and provides the client with practice in learning to handle this the most archetypical life dilemma. Whatever the client's specific problem may be, it, in one way or another, comes down to his capacity to handle love and its disappointment, and therapy provides a gymnasium for working out on that very issue. We can ask, is this not exactly what Anna O did with Brewer and, perhaps, what other (nearly all female) patients did with Freud. Whatever the specific value of the cathartic method or the transference analysis method or Rogers' empathic reflection method, all of which seem to get results, all involve the client in entering into a situation where feelings of love will be aroused (as Shlein points out) and, in the tenderest manner, uncompromisingly frustrated. Is this not just the set of conditions that replicates life's fundamental dilemma and provides the client with the conditions in which to learn to cope? The client's own ability to love is stimulated by the modelling of the therapist and the therapist also models the restraint of that love, keeping it consistently within 'professional boundaries'. Is this not an excellent environment in which to strengthen character and, in particular, to learn to sublimate one's instinctive energy, even so far as to make one into the kind of altruistic and philanthropic character illustrated by Pappenheim and Taft, people who were not only 'cured' in the sense of 'restored to social normality' but rather revolutionised to a point where their consciousness of others was actually higher than that of the average person? From this perspective, therapy emerges as an education of character that moves people in the direction of becoming more loving beings capable of handling the disappointment that that brings and capable of extending their love beyond the scope of the average person.

Grief and Contrition

When a client reflects honestly upon his history he is likely to find material that causes dismay. Some of it may be difficult to face. Initially there may be a tendency to become angry at others, at the world in general, or at God, however conceived. Life has been frustrating. Frustration brings up energy and an impulse to action. In the course of responding to these frustrations a person has done things. Many of the things done are likely to have been ill-advised (cf. Brazier 1997). Furthermore, a realistic assessment will show that although life is frustrating it is also supporting. The client is alive. Somehow he has come through. For this to have happened he has to have had support. Resources were made available to him every day one way or another. The sun rose each morning. Food was found. While we tend to be fixated upon the things that went wrong, we neglect to notice the myriad things that went right that kept our life venture from foundering. Further, when we look in detail we find that there have been innumerable incidents in which we have received benefit from others. Some of these are impersonal, as in the fact that food was cultivated all over the world and transported, packaged and distributed that eventually made its way onto our plate and kept us alive. Some are more personal, such as the fact that a member of our family cooked the food and fed it to us when we were young. The human infant is dependent and cannot manage without considerable input from others. We have all been a burden to others. Our very existence has given them work and inconvenience. We have not always responded to their efforts with gratitude or even acknowledgement, let alone done anything commensurate in return. Often enough, the disappointment of love that others have had to suffer and wrestle with has been of our making. Not that we have necessarily been malicious, but we have been blind.

Often the enormity of one's debt to another only becomes apparent to oneself when that other is lost. Grief and contrition may go together. In any case, object centred work is, after the initial level of exploration has been achieved, likely in many instances to lead to the kind of reassessment that precipitates contrite feelings that may be acute and painful. In Japan, this type of work is called Naikan (Krech 2001). It tends to lead people to an enhanced sense of gratitude, and appreciation of what others have done for one that may at first be unsettling. As Erich Fromm remarked, "The insane person or the dreamer fails completely in having an objective view of the world outside; but all of us are more or less insane, more of less asleep; all of us have an un-objective view of the world, one which is distorted by our narcissistic orientation." (Fromm 1957/1995, p.93). The ubiquity of selfishness does not, however, negate the primacy of love.

Earlier in this book we looked at how false guilt may hamper a life. At this stage we have to consider how real guilt not faced also hampers it. I do not mean, necessarily, the kind of guilt where a client has performed a crime for which they have never been prosecuted. I mean rather the commonplace guilt or debt that we all carry but seldom acknowledge. This has the effect of dulling our esteem. Paradoxically, an emphasis upon self-entitlement tends to make this worse. When we appreciate our health, our food, the company of our friends, the fact that we live in a country at peace (if we do), that the sun shines, as all being special things worthy of gratitude, then the quotient of esteem in our life is, by definition, much higher. We love more fluently. When we are self concerned the opposite occurs. Fromm thinks that "Love is not primarily a relationship to a specific person; it is an attitude, and orientation of character which determines the relatedness of a person to the world as a whole." (Fromm 1957/1995, p.36). The argument of this book is that it is both. All instances of specific esteem are capable of enhancing a person's ability to love. If we come to esteem many things, including all the little things of daily life, we shall have a vibrant loving life.

At the same time, it is easy to see that there are factors in our society that impede us doing so. The rise of individualism has not only cut people off from one another, it has created an ambiance in which it is necessary to justify oneself. This turns the establishment not just of an independent, but also a justified self into an important goal. In a situation where every one of us consumes more than we create and causes much inconvenience at least to others every day just by being part of society and having normal human needs, this has to lead to distortion. The modern person tends to view with horror Kierkegaard's recipe of "remorse, repentance and confession" (Kierkegaard 1961, p.34) not so much because he sees it as gloomy as because he is so strongly invested in the idea that one should live in such a way that occasion for such things not arise, just as he believes that love is something upon which the beatitude should ever and unremittingly shine. However, the real world is not like that and what an other centred approach does is to tenderly encourage us into a more painstakingly objective investigation of the facts of our situation. Paradoxical as it may seem, beyond the pain of remorse lies the enhancement of esteem that allows the current of love to flow once again. A not uncommon remark of clients who have done Naikan work, at the end of much weeping and reflection upon how much they have received, how little given, is 'I've got my mother back,' or some equal expression of how facing the reality of the imbalance in the relationship and feeling the feelings appropriate to one's part in the matter leads to renewed esteem and a clearing away of tension that has dulled that relationship, and, by extension, all one's relations for many years.

Esteem Between Therapist and Client

Modelling and Imitation
Esteem is associated with learning. On one occasion late in his life I met Carl Rogers and we conversed. I asked him if there was anything he would change in his theories set out over the preceding years, now that he had hindsight. He said that he was broadly happy with the point of view that he had expressed in his books, but then added that perhaps he had under-estimated the importance of modelling. People learn from one another. They imitate.

I also think that this is important. People learn in many ways, but imitation is certainly an important one. It is particularly obvious in adolescence. The teenager has heroes. He imitates them. He tries out their way of walking and talking, their gestures, facial expressions, voice tone and phrases. He imitates their dress. He tries it on for size. Some of these 'fads' may be fickle, but they exemplify a basic way in which human's extend their repertoire. We imitate those we esteem. Couples grow more like each other. People may even come to resemble their dog. Esteem leads to learning. Imitation may be a form of flattery, but it is also a form of love.

The fact that people learn by imitating those they esteem does not mean that the therapist should in some self-conscious way set herself up as model for the client. Doing so is likely to be counter-productive. Awareness that one is being imitated tends to generate self-consciousness and this is a disturbance to the natural flow in a person's way of being. As a third party, a researcher, say, one can see that clients do grow to be more like their therapists, no matter how non-directive the therapist is trying to be. In fact, such imitation is probably more likely to occur when the therapist is non-directive, which, ironically, may account for some of the success of non-directive therapy. We imitate what we sense to be genuine in the other and self-conscious modelling is not genuine, unless what the imitator wants is himself to be a model (which is why people do imitate celebrities). Modern society has unfortunately become infected with a great deal of this kind of artificiality, but it does not yield any depth of emotional satisfaction.

Response Learning

Esteem also leads to a different kind of learning: response learning. In any interaction with somebody who matters to us we are put on the spot. The other relates to us and we have to find a response. Sometimes the response we find amounts to a new deployment of some element of our existing repertoire. Sometimes we have to come up with something that feels entirely new. We feel an obligation not to let the other person down, not to let the thread of conversation drop. Or, it may be, that we feel compelled to attend. One of the most important lessons we ever learn in life, if we do learn it, is to listen. Our ability to attend in depth to another is something that seems to have infinite capacity for refinement.

In his reminiscences, Rogers talks about an occasion when he learnt something important. He was working in a counselling project for young people. He would sometimes see the parents and try to help them to find new ways of handling their youngsters' behaviour. With one particular family he felt that he was getting nowhere when, one day, the mother, we'll call her Mrs G:

> "turned and asked 'Do you ever take adults for counseling here?' Puzzled, I replied that sometimes we did. Whereupon she returned to the chair she had just left and began to pour out a story of the deep difficulties between herself and her husband and her great desire for some kind of help. I was bowled over. What she was telling me bore no resemblance to the neat history I had drawn from her. I scarcely knew what to do, but mostly I listened." (Rogers 1980, p. 36).

This was Rogers as a young, relatively inexperienced counsellor. What he himself understands himself as having taken from this was principally the value of listening.

> "This was a vital learning for me. I had followed her lead rather than mine. I had listened instead of trying to nudge her toward a diagnostic understanding I had already reached. It was a far more personal relationship, and not nearly so 'professional'. Yet the results spoke for themselves." (*ibid*. p.37, original italics).

Listening is an important aspect of esteem, of love, and Rogers had learnt something important about it. It was to become a much more central element in his approach from then on.

However, there is an additional aspect to this example that should not be overlooked. This was a special incident. Rogers was taken by surprise by this mother's request. One can imagine that, in that circumstance, he was at his edge on that occasion.

His adrenalin level was high. One can imagine that this would not have been the case the next time a mother, Mrs P, the following week, said to him, 'Do you see adults for counselling?' By the time he has seen several, he will be completely at ease, in his 'comfort zone' (Jeffers 1987), and he will, perhaps, say, "Of course, please sit down and tell me your story," and the effect might be different. On the first occasion, in the story above, Rogers was challenged. He came up with something because he had some genuine concern for Mrs. G. He went slightly beyond the call of duty. This is in itself significant in two ways.

Firstly, it is significant in that Rogers himself was learning. He was finding a new response. Jacob Moreno had a terminology for this. He would say that the first time something happens it is 'spontaneity', but once it has happened a few times it has become part of the 'cultural conserve' (Moreno 1977). We each have a 'conserve' of strategies that have worked before. Moreno had a slightly mystical idea about therapy. Spontaneity is creativity. Creation is what God does. For Moreno, moments of spontaneity were divine intervention.

Secondly, the fact that Rogers went beyond the call of duty will not have been lost on Mrs. G, even though she will probably never remark upon it. It is concrete evidence of Rogers' esteem for her that will not be there to the same degree when he invites Mrs P to speak. Mrs P will get the message that 'this is all part of the service' which is a weaker message than Mrs G received.

These observations are inconvenient. It would be convenient if we could simply learn a method that works in all cases. Rogers learnt the importance of listening and ever after was an advocate of careful listening and this is without doubt important and a way of demonstrating esteem, but listening as a matter of course is not what happened with Mrs G, and this difference created something special, "It was a far more personal relationship" (p.37) and "she was the first client I ever had who continued to keep in occasional touch with me for years afterward, until her boy was doing well in college." (p.36). This special factor would not be there with our hypothetical Mrs P. Nor, indeed was it actually there with the many real Mrs Ps who did come along as Rogers developed his listening method.

There is more. Rogers' remark "until her boy was doing well in college" is also revealing. Not only did the specialness of the incident create a bond between Rogers and Mrs G, it was a particular kind of bond, a bond that had a third party in view. Whether they spoke of him or not on that critical occasion, the bond between Rogers and Mrs G had Mrs G's son in view. The whole incident occurred because they shared a concern - we can say 'esteem' - for the boy. That is what it was all about, after all. A self psychologist might think that Mrs G capitalized upon the meeting with her son's therapist to get something for herself. I do not think that that is what matters to her most. What matters to the mother is her son. Her own problem and its solution are instrumental. She must solve her problem in order to be any use to the son. This is what makes her risk her dignity by bearing her soul to Rogers. Such a personal exposure, however, does create a bond.

This is a most inconvenient fact for the therapy profession. At an instinctive level, if the kind of bond that is likely to be genuinely therapeutic is established, then it itself involves demands that go well beyond what the boundaries of therapy permit. Rogers cannot go home with Mrs G and become a surrogate uncle to the son, at Mrs G's elbow whenever she needs emotional support. Yet, at some level, that is what she now must want. Therapy, therefore, has its boundaries and these become frustrations for the client and, perhaps, for the therapist. In the good case, they become frustrations to the client's love that help the client to grow. They demand a development of character. Just as Rogers had to come up with a response learning when Mrs G put him on the spot and asked for counselling, so Mrs G must find a response to the circumstance that although she has now found this sympathetic and caring man who shares her deep concern and esteem for her son, she cannot have him in her life in anything more than an extremely restricted way. Love has been born and must now be immediately disappointed. Such is therapy and such is life. She restricts herself to writing to Rogers 'occasionally'. Her self-restraint in this respect is also part of her esteem, her respect for Rogers, and her concern to keep things proper and not encroach 'beyond duty' more than he had done, thus keeping everything safe for all parties while still acknowledging that something beyond the ordinary had happened, something sufficiently beyond the ordinary that it was still alive in Rogers' mind decades later when he wrote *A Way of Being*. The optimum distance was achieved by an action that lifted the relationship beyond the (over-distanced) routine and so Rogers' work with Mrs G became a memorable work of art where his work with Mrs P and her successors did not.

So there are two types of learning in therapy. One is imitative and the other responsive and the two are mutually supportive and reinforcing. They are powerful when they occur in circumstances that bring the individual close to their edge. However, neither operates independently of the process of esteem. Nor are they particular to therapy. They are part of the normal process of life. Therapy exploits these facts, but the more self-consciously it does so, the less effective it is likely to be.

Techniqueless Therapy?

The Impotence of Technique
It might initially seem from this that a practical implication of an other centred approach would be that that there were really no particular techniques that would yield real therapy, since all hangs upon the regard. Therapist and client meet, spend time together and must do something. There is no particular activity that will guarantee a successful outcome. There is no formula of

words that the therapist must say without which therapy will not take place; no action that must be performed. There is no efficient means. Even though we have above set out a protocol for an object related way of working, there is no more guarantee of work done to that protocol being any more immune to routinization (over-distancing) than any other.

Therapy is an intense relationship. The client is bound to have feelings for the therapist and the therapist for the client. Calling these 'transference' and 'counter-transference' may occasionally be useful in helping one to understand origins, but understanding origins is no royal road to health. A person can be well aware of why they are sick and still remain so. Knowing that one hates all men because of what one's father did to one may expose the insanity of blaming all for what one person did, but it does not necessarily stop one from doing it.

Again, therapy is a place where the client declares what he thinks about various aspects of his life and these ways of thinking reveal something of the esteem that he has for this or that aspect of his family and social milieu and his physical and economic circumstances. This esteem in turn gives evidence of how and to what extent he is able to fulfil his love drive or feel frustrated in it. The therapist and client might discuss different ways in which the client might think about some of these significant others and we might sometimes call this type of discussion 'cognitive restructuring', but it will not be by learning a technique of thinking primarily that the client will re-evaluate his world.

Understanding the origins, restructuring ways of thinking, adopting new behaviours, carrying out 'homework' tasks, and so on may all form parts of therapy and none of them are useless, but it is truer to say that they are vehicles for a relationship within which the client relearns the art of loving than to think of them as primary therapeutic agents. A reformed character may find some such elements handy, but the reform itself comes through the working out of the process of esteem.

Rogers was deeply concerned about the inconvenient implications of the technique question. He had a strongly empirical turn of mind. He wanted to see what actually happened in therapy and what caused what. However, studying what therapists did in detail "led to a heavy emphasis on technique - the so-called non-directive technique" (Rogers 1980, p.37), and "we became heavily conscious of the techniques that the counselor or therapist was using. We became expert in analyzing, in very minute detail, the ebb and flow of the process in each interview, and we gained a great deal from that microscopic study. *But this tendency to focus on the therapist's responses had appalling consequences...* The whole approach came, in a few years, to be known as a technique. 'Nondirective therapy,' it was said, 'is the technique of reflecting the client's feelings.'"(*ibid.* p.139, my italics) Rogers says that he was shocked by seeing his work taken in this way, yet acknowledged that the appeal of many of the therapies that were being invented and written about at that time was that "A technological society has been delighted to have found a technology by which people's behavior can be shaped, even without their knowledge and approval, towards gaols selected by therapists or by society." (p.140).

So Rogers was closely interested in the minutiae of interaction between therapist and client, but fundamentally did not see himself as developing a technique. Rather he saw that what was really powerful was the orientation or attitude or philosophy of the therapist and this had broad implications. "I was finding that this new-found trust in my client and his capacity for exploring and resolving his problems reached out uncomfortably into other areas. If I trusted my clients, why didn't I trust my students? If this was fine for the individual in trouble, why not for a staff group facing problems? I found that I had embarked not on a new *method* of therapy, but a sharply different *philosophy* of living and relationships." (Rogers 1980, pp.37-38). Rogers found that his colleagues were, however, much happier and more at ease with the idea of a technique than a philosophy.

Esteem theory suggests a somewhat similar outlook to that of Rogers. It is not that it does not enable one to devise techniques that are congruent with its philosophy, but it does emphasise that the technique may not, at the end of the day, be what really matters or makes the difference. Rogers listened to Mrs G, but more fundamentally Rogers cared enough about Mrs G and her son to listen. I suggest that this instance of being loved enabled Mrs G to love more, and, in particular, to love her son more. As we have already suggested, listening that is simply matter of course may have much less impact. It is not listening *per se*, so much as what listening speaks of. If we listen because listening is what one does in a caring intimate relationship, but do so without caring, without actually having such a relationship, then it becomes a hollow and meaningless charade. As professionals we try to avoid having to talk about such things as love, but it is still the love that matters in the end. A profession wants to have techniques because they can then be presented as being a body of knowledge and expertise and that is what gives a profession its legitimacy, but in the domain of psychotherapy a technique is generally something that in its native state would be an indicator of love deployed professionally by people who do not do it for love, but as part of a routine protocol. This is, as Rogers forcefully pointed out, 'appalling'. Therapy is an art not a science. What it deals in cannot be measured. Therapy theory has gone a long way in the scientific age by measuring indicators that commonly accompany the unmeasurable element that does matter, but the mistaking of the indicator for what it is thought to signify has also caused great confusion.

Technique Nonetheless

What then can we say for technique? Several things. While there is truth in the idea of 'techniquelessness', that cannot mean that there are not things that client and therapist can do together that are suggested by and in line with the basic philosophy of the approach being here outlined. The problem is firstly that these are legion and secondly, as we have said at length, that they are no use when they lack the substance provided by real esteem.

We have already spoken earlier about object related work and this clearly has value. If the therapist spends time helping the client to investigate the significant objects of his world this yields insight into the constellations of esteem that govern his life and provides opportunities for the therapist to herself obtain some regard growing to esteem for those objects herself, albeit at a remove. It is a more or less universal attribute of love that it esteems those things that the beloved esteems. While we may, therefore, legitimately call 'object related work' a proper technique of the other centred approach, the reason that it is so is that it replicates one of the fundamental ways that people express love. Therapy technique, then, includes a number of such replicas. They are nothing in themselves, but become something when filled out with the appropriate sentiments and intentions that make them real and these are all species of love.

Therapy technique is always contextual. The skilled therapist creates new technique as he goes along. Some aspects of context are broad. These include factors relating to the culture. Some of the things that Freud did do not work today because this is not early twentieth century Vienna. Martin Stanton, writes about Ferenczi's approach to technique as follows:

"Ferenczi's alternative is to accept that psychoanalysis is bound to operate within numerous interlocking power structures which it can neither easily negotiate nor subvert. People come to you as patients looking for doctors who 'know' and expecting some 'active' response. They are going to regress to infantile dependence and need some support. To argue then for a strategy which will totally frustrate such expectations and demands could be taken as cruel rejection, no matter how 'enlightened' the intent. Similarly, to relax people in the analytical session to the point where they come to see the analyst as the good breast machine that pumps out a regular 'fix' deprives them of both independence and the chance to discover what really oppresses them. Ferenczi therefore argues for multiple and varied psychoanalytic techniques, which can be applied flexibly according to the context." (Stanton 1990, p.61).

The fundamental question, therefore, is, what is most loving in the particular situation? The answer is not necessarily easy to cognize, but will in practice arise through the trial and error of the relationship as much as from the fact that the therapist does have a stock of techniques - her bag of toys.

We have to see the techniques that the therapist has command of not so much as the efficient driving force of therapy as rather sometimes useful elements of human interaction in situations where the client does have a tale to tell and problems to elucidate. Sometimes a technique may help a client to tell their tale. If I give my client a sheet of flip-chart paper, he may be able to draw his family tree much more effectively than he could have described it in words. If I give him a box of small objects and a sand pit he may be able to sculpt it. He may even go on to manipulate the toys in ways that represent existing and hoped for changes in relationships as he discerns them. All of this is technique and all of it is useful up to a point. It is loving to provide the other with the means to do something if one has that means to hand. None of this means, however, that, in the last analysis it is not the love that makes the difference, nor that the technique of diagrammatic representation or that of play therapy are of any real power without it. The important thing, therefore, is to grasp the relationship between these different elements of the therapeutic situation and to form a sense of the synthetic whole that they compose and to see how the central principle at work in this synthesis is always love within its frustrating boundary and that the primary manifestation of love is the varieties of esteem.

We should also pause a moment to reflect upon Stanton's 'however enlightened'. There is a danger in psychotherapy theory that rather than focussing upon what is most therapeutic for the client in their circumstances, one finds the theory distorted by ideals that the therapist believes to be proper for society. It is not, however, the therapist's task to try to reform the society via the client nor to attempt to make the client into an example of a 'better' kind of citizen ideally fitted for the 'better' world that the therapist wishes to see come about. In other words therapy can be distorted by 'political correctness' or social idealism. Thus, many therapists may hold democratic political ideals, but it is not their duty to force a 'democratic' style of relationship upon the client if that is not what the client wants. To do so would be unsympathetic exploitation. Love takes a million forms and always relates to the real life situation. There can be almost nothing in the range of possible human behaviour that could not be an act of love under some circumstance or other. That would, in fact, follow from the basic axiom of esteem theory. If the drive to love is the central and most fundamental element in our psychic make-up then it would follow that all the things that human beings are capable of doing are or can be at some time or other servants of love. That they can also be used for other purposes does not change this and I would want to argue that even when they are so used, there is an ultimate loving aim still in the picture, however remote.

All this suggests that therapeutic technique can be extremely varied while keeping the emphasis upon the fact that the really therapeutic ingredient is not the technique itself. Techniques may be things that simply have practical utility in helping the client to tell his story or to elucidate some part of it, or they may set up situations where there is an opportunity to discover something, to rehearse a plan, to use the 'conserve' in new ways, or whatever. Broadly, many techniques are moderately useful, but, even though the attention of client and therapist may be wholly absorbed in them they are only a medium.

Let us take psychodrama as an example. This is one of the most elaborate and absorbing of technical systems. The trainee psycho-dramatist must learn about role theory and spontaneity, about tele and catharsis, about warm-ups, action and sharing, getting into role and de-roling, scene setting, doubling, surplus reality, play-back, and many other wonderful elements. However, it is a notable fact that if you take as a beginning psychodrama therapy trainee somebody who knows a certain amount about theatre, perhaps, but nothing about therapy, it will typically take several years to turn him into a psycho-dramatist, whereas if you take a skilled psychotherapist as your student he will acquire the art in a much shorter time. This is because it does not really take very long to acquire a set of techniques and learn how they work with one another, but it does take a long time to gain the necessary sensitivity to discern what is required in a therapeutic situation, irrespective of whether the medium is psychodrama or whatever. That said, and it is generally true, there are also some people with no therapy training who are nonetheless 'naturals' and able to exhibit a therapeutic sensitivity simply as a result of their loving nature and positive esteem for the world around them and the beings that inhabit it.

In general, therefore, for an other centred practitioner, any technique might be appropriate, but no technique is going to be regarded as a solution in itself. Techniques are aids. They are like tools. It is not the tools that make a cabinet, it is the carpenter, and the skilled carpenter may make use of many tools, can readily adapt to using other ones, and can even make do with minimum equipment if he has to. Or, we can even say that techniques are a little like toys. The therapist has a toy chest and has many interesting things in it and may invite the client to play with some of them. What matters is not really the particular game that they play together, though some games do have intrinsic interest and some may appeal to a particular client more than others, but what is more crucial is the esteem that the therapist has for the client and the esteem that the client comes to have for the therapist and for the significant others that inhabit his world.

It follows that therapy could take some forms that are remote from what people stereotypically think of. Perhaps therapy could come through reading Homer together, or through going fell walking, or working together to prepare a meal for friends. Youth workers are well aware that the classical method of sitting down on two chairs facing each other and attempting the 'talking cure' simply does not work for many adolescents and anthropologists know that it is unknown in many cultures, but that those cultures are not devoid of pathways by which people become more mature, better socially adjusted, recover from trauma or phobia, or resolve issues that they have with their significant others, living and dead. Each culture has its methods. In the sociable milieu of Italy, one may do therapy over dinner whereas in the businesslike ambiance of America a more clinical environment may work better. In my own early career I was a psychiatric social worker before I was a psychotherapist. As a PSW one had a wider range of ways of engaging the client as options. The aim is, however, not that of having as big a range of options as possible, but to use whatever options one does have in an appropriate and sensitive way that evidences (and, therefore, incidentally, also models) genuine esteem.

Staleness and Technique
We may be helped in our exploration of the relationship between technique and therapeutic effect by returning to a comparison with what happens in art. Artistic endeavours involve two distinct objects that are the two sides of the mimesis. One object

is the matter depicted, whether symbolically or directly. On the other side is the art object that the artist creates. In the case of music we might follow Aristotle in taking emotion as its object. Certainly music has a quality of pure form that is sometimes envied by practitioners of other arts. Some poets, including some who have achieved fame, seem to have concerned themselves more with the 'music' of their compositions than with the meaning. In part this is because all arts sometimes want to make emotion their true object. However, although the 'music' is a highly significant constitutive element in poetry it is truer to regard that 'music' as part of the technique than the substance of the art, whereas in music itself it is obviously the music that counts. We can see that what is technique and what is substance varies with the case. Similarly, in therapy, sometimes emotion is the subject matter, but by no means always. Generally emotion is an accompaniment to life, not its purpose or main theme. Coombes (1953, pp.17-22) provides examples of instances where poets have sacrificed sense for music and others where the two work together. The art appreciator is going to enjoy seeing an example of good technique. It has an intrinsic value. However, this is really a subsidiary matter. In good art technique should be used in the service of the purpose of the particular work, rarely showcased in its own right.

Art grasps our esteem and in doing so educates, reshapes, challenges, and reconstellates it. It is in art's nature to push toward esteem's limits. In pressing the limits of esteem it implicitly seeks to reach toward the solution of the human dilemma of continuing to live in an environment resistant to love. Some art, therefore, shocks, in a very similar manner to that in which dark humour shocks. In fact, art and humour are attempting something very similar. They have more in common than is generally realized. This becomes more obviously true in the case of modern art, or, perhaps we should say, art confronted with the modern world. T.S.Eliot's poetry, for instance, frequently hovers on the edge of black humour and Eliot often wrote nonsense verse in his spare time, which is another echo of modern fragmentation. Eliot and Ezra Pound set in motion a movement in modern poetry that, in the aftermath of the first world war, "spearheaded Modernism in Britain and provoked an important battle between what was popular and what was authentically original." (Padel 2007, p.9) When an art has become non-original, it has become dominated by technique, replacing what was once fresh and substantial. What is substance when it first occurs, becomes technique by imitation. This is why some therapies, like Neuro-Linguistic Programing (NLP) which are unabashedly based on imitating what leading therapists have done, often seem so lacking in depth. That kind of imitation is not at all what Aristotle had in mind. Similarly, there are a range of therapies and personal growth techniques available today that attempt to replicate what Carl Rogers did, but in a completely formulaic manner. This kind of thing has its vogue, but really is a trivialisation of what therapy is about.

This does not mean that something repeated many times necessarily becomes technique; ritual or the performance of a play in a long run by an accomplished actor need never necessarily become stale. It is the performance by rule in which a relationship of true esteem never arises or has been lost that becomes stale. For the accomplished actor, even if this is the hundredth night that he has performed Othello, it is still fresh and new for a unique audience.

For instance, to return to poetry, it is true that, generally speaking, concrete language is more vivid than abstraction, a principle that also applies to therapy. It is also true that introducing the concrete often means noticing specific details of a situation: 'the campion growing between the cow parsley', rather than 'the summer flowers'. But why? The reason is that reference to specific detail gives evidence of close observation and close observation gives evidence of esteem (as, the lover knows the colour of his beloved's eyes). However, to then serve up 'evidence' in cases where the esteem is actually lacking is not art, it is a frame-up. A poem is not a list. Modernism, at its worst, has produced many poems that are little more. A belief has grown up that the task of poetry is that of presenting accurate images of the world, often one after another, like a series of exhibits, without any real sense of why. How has this self-deception happened? Louis Menand points out that "empiricism... is in fact one of the sponsors of modern aesthetic theory." (Menand 1987, p.31). We are, in part, dealing with a modern problem to do with the distorting effect of the prestige of science, but beyond that, we are dealing with a more general problem of producing the sign for something rather than the thing itself. The thing itself is generally love in some form or other, but if all that arrives are it's common accompaniments it is like a meal with no main course.

Anything can be corrupted. If something is commonly a sign of something else, one can start to produce the sign and forget its original meaning. Yet the sign is empty on its own. One can take even the most alive and vibrant act of a master and reproduce it as stale technique for use by apprentices. This is one of the reasons that teaching therapy is difficult. One does not become a great therapist by imitating Carl Rogers or Sigmund Freud in such a way. It is only by picking up the spirit of what such pioneers were attempting that one may produce genuine therapy, just as one will not become a true artist by making shallow imitations of Renoir, but only by being infected with the spirit that moved him, or rather, the spirit that moves oneself. It is true that you will have to learn some skill with the brushes too, but genuine inspiration is quite different from merely technical imitation. I hope it is now clear how there is a world of difference between imitation in this stale sense and the mimesis that Aristotle talks of as the essence of art.

As soon as one does become so inspired one does need some technique. It is just that the technique must serve the substance not substitute for it and the substance in therapy, as in art, revolves around true esteem and therefore love. We can see from this history of poetry, however, that the art needs to be continually reinvented and can never be reduced to a formula or set of protocols. It lives in relation to a tradition, "Yet if the only form of tradition, of handing down, consisted in following the ways of the immediate generation before us in a blind or timid adherence to its successes, 'tradition' should be positively discouraged. We have seen many such simple currents soon lost in the sand; and novelty is better than repetition. Tradition is a matter of much wider significance. It cannot be inherited, and if you want it you must obtain it by great labour." (Eliot 1932/1999, p.14).

The idea that the following of protocols will of itself effect therapeutic change is nonsense. The real human beings who become therapists and who must operate such procedures achieve therapeutic affect, if they do so, by injecting something real into the situation which can never be prescribed by the protocol.

Part Six

In Conclusion, A Glimpse of the
Meaning of Life

Jacob Moreno feared that modern man was becoming a machine. God was dead or dying, and, for Moreno, God meant creativity and spontaneity. He saw the role of psychotherapy as being to restore the fullness of life which to him meant the restoration of spontaneity and creativity. These he understood to be the eruption of the divine in the midst of the mundane. The spontaneous creative will that restores fullness to life is love and its mark is esteem. However, we cannot over-look the fact that machines do dominate modern life and we who love and esteem machinery inevitably become more like it. However, machines do not love.

In the psychotherapy world a number of philosophies, each with its own perspective on life and culture, contend. They also seek respectability in the context of this modern society. We see the analytic views of Freud and his followers, including those of many of his critics, contending with the notion that what is actually happening is a learning process, either behavioural learning or cognitive learning, and both those ideas in competition with humanistic approaches that try to put the subjectivity of the person back at the centre of concern in a more positive (or, overly optimistic, depending upon your perspective) manner than the analysts do. Again, all of these approaches are not infrequently viewed by the layman as so many species of mysticism if not obscurantism while a vast repository of understanding of the human condition lies in works not produced in or for the academy or the clinic, but in the literary and spiritual traditions of the world.

Nonetheless, psychology does contribute to the changes that go on in our culture as well as deriving from them, and the arts are even more inseparable from it. In this book we have examined the close relations between all three. There are inherent difficulties for any project based in the humanities operating in our contemporary world. It may be a sign of our times that poetry is today so little regarded. Even though most Sunday newspapers have a supplement devoted to the arts, it is now rare to find coverage of poetry in it. Perhaps I am wrong in considering poetry to occupy a special position in culture. Perhaps its eclipse is just part of the normal cycle of things and in fifty years it will be poetry that everyone talks about while, say, painting is disregarded. However, there does seem to me to be a core role for poetry. At the root of Western culture lies Homer. Then comes Christianity with its lyrical book. Poetry is the stuff of epic and we no longer seem to have one. We no longer have much sense of what our culture is or what it is for, except inasmuch as we have come to think that it is some kind of machine. I think this decline is associated with the loss of poetry from our national consciousness. What poetry there is nowadays has become a kind of cottage industry with its 'working poets' associated with a rather proletarian vision of morality, glorifying the commonplace. This is not bad in itself, but we are surely capable of more. An associated deficit, noted by David Smail (1997, p.162) is that the twentieth century (and the twenty first is so far no better) failed to produce any examples of great tragic theatre. When we remember the pivotal part that Aristotle attributed to poetry and tragedy as the high points of any culture and look at the scene today we have reason to be disquieted.

Therapy is a kind of poetry and it certainly addresses tragedies. Therapy is the enterprise of two or more people exploring what is most important to at least one of them and expressing it in words and actions, but primarily words, that do justice to it and suggest its relevance to what is most meaningful in the life of the individual. It commonly, but not always, has a curative intention inasmuch as it is provoked by a sense that all is not well. Often enough what is not well with the individual reflects what is not well with the collective. I find myself in agreement with Eliot that "the culture of the individual is dependent upon the culture of a group or class, and the culture of the group or class is dependent upon the culture of the whole society." (Eliot 1948/1962, p.21), but I also note that we live in an age in which the 'whole society' is substantially represented by the state which has become such a powerful human machine that the culture of groups and individuals is atrophied. Culture is a function of the patterning of esteem. The prestige of ideas of 'freedom and democracy' while advanced with the good intention of liberating the individual have to a substantial degree cut him loose from such patterning and, in the process, tended to undermine the conditions that support esteem altogether. We are now expected to admire celebrities who are expected to behave badly. This is not a recipe for social betterment.

Psychotherapy has grown up during the period in which these shifts in the spirit of the times have been taking place. On the one hand psychotherapy has sought to support the humanity of the individual. On the other it has also often supported him in declaring his independence of the structures that support his humanity. At the same time, therapy has itself been invaded by the dominant ethos. It has become substantially bureaucratised and regulated and is increasingly dedicated to the quest for procedures and protocols that can be 'scientifically' validated at a level that makes the actual human beings who operate the protocol irrelevant, so that actual therapists may be reduced to a more and more machinelike status. "Psychotherapy is in constant danger of succumbing to the diseases that it exists to cure." (Brazier 2003b, p.285)

However, as ever, there is another way of understanding this. As we live in a machine esteeming age, it is perhaps necessary that the myth that the therapist offers the client often can be one that chimes with this dominant one. If the therapist can tell the client that there is scientific evidence for a procedure, then the client may be more willing to play and when the client and therapist start to play together with some third object in view, mythical or otherwise, empathy and mutual esteem grow. The myth disguises itself in the garb of science. Therapy is about love and esteem, and love is infinitely flexible at the level of signs, being willing to deliver whatever tokens the beloved finds charming. If it helps that these bear the label 'science' or 'code validated', then that may be what is used. It is the nature of love to adapt. What the beloved esteems, the lover learns to esteem.

"The therapist emerges, in all evaluations of psychotherapy, as crucial to its success. He is not a vehicle for valuable theories of human functioning, rather, the theories are a vehicle for him. They bring him to his patients confident that he has the expertise to help them, prepared to invade their privacy and willing to offer himself as a model, guide and friend." (Mair 1997, p.92) This means that it is the therapist's human qualities that matter and these are his various patterns of esteem, his ways of loving.

In this book I have not sought to refute any of the currently prevalent approaches to psychotherapy. I have tried, rather, to get down a level to see what may be going on underneath each of them. What are the real agents? The other centred approach advanced here draws heavily upon what I learnt from Carl Rogers, yet it finds itself to a surprising degree in accord with the basic structure of ideas advanced by Freud, asserts that there is a learning process at the core of psychotherapy, and does so with less offence to 'common sense' or perennial wisdom than is common in this field. In one sense, therefore, this is an exercise in integration. This is all achieved by the simple expedient of restoring love to a central role in our understanding of what it is to be a person who is inevitably a person in a world. This other centred approach thus goes some distance toward reconciling the analytical and the artistic, the humanistic and the scientific. It also extends to other fields. In cultural matters it similarly offers some prospect of reconciliation between the classical, the romantic and the existentialist which do present a somewhat parallel set of distinctions to those found in the specifically therapeutic world (Brazier D. 2008). Similar fundamental principles apply to all aspects of human culture. Everywhere people are selfish, yet under it all, love is the true driving force. This simple principle proves to have a sturdy unifying potential, provides a remarkably fecund spring from which new thinking about method arises and brings psychotherapy back into line with a range of wisdom that is recognisable to the ordinary person. Whether it can find favour in our machine idolatrous culture may be a different matter.

Nor of themselves will self-actualization, or enhanced consciousness or awareness emancipate us. The former may be a by-product that hardly need be noticed, and the latter may sometimes serve as an intermediate factor in the growth process, as it does in the mastery of any skill, but the goal, insofar as one may generalize it, is to be a more accomplished and consummate lover of the significant others in one's life, diverse or idiosyn-cratic as these may be, and if one is consumed by the ordinary day to day love of life, then one will not bother with thoughts of self, and if this orientation has become 'second nature', then one will not have a heightened awareness of it.

In sum, therefore, agreeing with Rogers on the power of empathy, congruence and unconditional positive regard to occasion constructive personality change, I am inclined to trace their effectiveness to the functioning of love and esteem as the strong force or drive in human life struggling with reality factors through which the secondary, but ubiquitous self-preservative drives come to form the pervasive 'weak force' of our existence, and to the need of the client for support and companionship along this obstacle filled road. The manifestations of love and esteem by the therapist for the client and for his significant others may take innumerable forms. Their genuine and skilful expression calls forth a like response. As the client also comes to esteem his world, so he becomes a fuller and more lovable human being, better able to love and more able to fare well through its vicissitudes, both its satisfactions and its disappointment. Applied to psychotherapy method, this line of thinking yields, in keeping with Rogers' original vision of 'client centred therapy', an other centred approach.

The human being is other orientated. In its most noble and affecting form this is love. Love in the real world entrains the satisfactions of esteem and the disappointments of non-consummation. Social and spiritual maturity come from the inner chemistry that follows upon these investments and their variable returns. In the mundane life we love others and must necessarily encounter their and our limitations, not least the necessary limit upon our knowledge that leaves both self and other ultimately, and often even proximately, as mysteries. While our knowledge is limited, this mystery is infinite. To encounter the infinite mystery that is the ground of love and to bear the suffering occasioned by its inevitable disappointments is spirituality and the return of such spirituality to the collective life in a manner beneficial, if challenging, to oneself and others is religion. We are thus inherently beings that worship. Much of our worship is, in practice, idolatry, love squandered on unworthy objects, but we can hardly help ourselves. Whether at the sublime or the mundane level, we live to love and we suffer as a result. To the extent that we keep faith through such travail we generate a more and more mature life. To the extent that we fail to do so we generate psychopathology. The task of therapy is to provide an arena in which we can turn our steps in a healthier direction. The task of spirituality is to place us before the sublime in a state of grace and support us in our response to its inaccessibility. Popular art celebrates our intuitive appreciation of the sublime, even if in forms that are kitsch. Great art restores our perception of the sublime even when the subject matter is mundane. Life is other centred: a mortal struggle with love and its disappointment.

Notes

1. Throughout this work, wherever the pronouns "he" or "she" are used, 'he or she' may be assumed. unless the context makes it explicit that a gendered issue is being discussed. When relations between complimentary pairs, such as therapist and client, are being discussed in the general case, the convention of making them of opposite gender will be adopted for clarity. The reader may again take it, however that what is being said applies equally whatever the sex of the two people may be unless the context explicitly indicates otherwise.

2. See also, C. Brazier 2009, Other Centred Therapy, London: O Books (in press at the time of writing)

3. Thus, Germain Lietaer (1990b), after reviewing the voluminous literature on CCT and PCA at that time still wrote, "Since 1965 not much work has been done on the level of theory building." (P.37)

4. A critical assessment of Rogers I & II can be found in Frankel & Sommerbeck 2005; for the case for saying that "Rogers did not alter his fundamental views", see Bozarth 1990; and for a brief summary of the history see Raskin 2005.

5. Shlien originally committed these thoughts to paper in a dicussion paper that was circulated within the University of Chicago Counseling Center in the early nineteen sixties, well before my own paper. Their appearance in book form however did not occur until 2003 so it does not seem that there was influence in either direction, though I did meet Shlien on a number of occasions at international gatherings.

6. See Lawrence 1976, and Weinstein & Weinstein 1993.

7. For an extensive exposition of how complex guilt feelings develop in children see Brazier C.J. 2009.

8. Amida Trust: http://www.amidatrust.com and http://www.buddhistpsychology.info

9. The term mitwelt is borrowed from existentialism and refers to the client's experiential world carried with them in imagination (from German mit = 'with', welt = 'world'). The term is useful in that it implies, correctly, that what is commonly referred to as a person's 'inner' world is not actually phenomenologically experienced as being in any literal sense 'inside'. If one thinks of one's (absent) mother, one imagines her, perhaps, somewhere in the room where one is, outside of one's own body space. The imagined other is 'with' but not 'inside' one. For further, see Brazier 1994.

10. A useful description of work to achieve optimum distance in a therapy session is provided by the focussing therapist, Mia Leijssen (Leijssen 1993).

Bibliography

1. Ackroyd P. 1984. *T.S.Eliot*. London: Sphere
2. Bates Y. & House R. 2003. *Ethically Challenged Professions: Enabling innovation and diversity in psychotherapy and counselling*. Ross-on-Wye: PCCS Books
3. Bloom H. 1997. *The Anxiety of Influence: A theory of poetry*. Oxford: Oxford University Press
4. Bozarth J 1990. "The essence of client-centered therapy". In Lietaer *et al*. 1990, pp.59-64
5. Brazier C. 2003. *Buddhist Psychology*. London: Constable
6. Brazier C. 2009. *Guilt*. O Books
7. Brazier D. 1991. *Eigenwelt and Gegenwelt*. Narborough, Leicestershire: Amida Trust Occasional paper
8. Brazier D. (Editor) 1993. *Beyond Carl Rogers: Towards a psychotherapy for the 21st century*. London: Constable.
9. Brazier D. 1993b. "The Necessary Condition is Love: Going beyond self in the person-centred approach". In Brazier 1993, pp.72-91
10. Brazier D. 1994. *Eigenwelt and Mitwelt*. Narborough, Leicestershire: Amida Trust Occasional paper
11. Brazier D. 1995 .*Zen Therapy*. London: Constable
12. Brazier D. 1997. *The Feeling Buddha*. London: Constable
13. Brazier D. 2001. *The New Buddhism*. London: Constable
14. Brazier D. 2003b. "The Future of Psychotherapy", in Bates & House 2003, pp.285-290.
15. Brazier D. 2008 "CBT in Historico-Cultual Perspective", in House & Loewenthal 2008, pp.72-76.
16. Brazier D. & Beech C. 1994. "Phenomenological Multi-Media Therapy", in Jones 1994, pp.149-164
17. Buber M. (translated by W. Kaufman) 1970. *I and Thou*. New York: Charles Scribner's Sons
18. Coombes H. 1953. *Literature and Criticism*. London: Penguin

19. Ehman 1968. "Personal Love" In Soble 1989, pp.254-271
20. Eliot T.S. 1932/1999. *Selected Essays*. London: Faber & Faber
21. Eliot T.S. 1948/1962. *Notes Towards the Definition of Culture*. London: Faber & Faber
22. Eliot T.S., edited by L. Rainey, 2005. *The Annotated Waste Land with Eliot's Contemporary Prose*. London: Yale University Press
23. Frankel M. & Sommerbeck L. 2005. "Two Rogers and Congruence: The emergnce of therapist-centered therapy and the demise of client-centered therapy". In Levitt 2005, pp.40-61.
24. Freud S. 1985. *Art and Literature: The Penguin Freud Library, volume 14*. London: Penguin
25. Freud S. 1991. *On Metapsychology: The Penguin Freud Library, Volume 11*. London: Penguin
26. Fromm E. 1957/1995 *The Art of Loving*. London: Harper Collins (originally George, Allen & Unwin 1957).
27. Grof S. & Grof J.H. 1977. *The Human Encounter with Death*. New York: E.P.Dutton Co.
28. Hamburger M. 1968. *The Truth of Poetry: Tensions in Modernist Poetry since Baudelaire*. London: Anvil Press Poetry
29. Harris J.R. 1998. *The Nurture Assumption: Why children turn out the way they do*. New York: Simon & Schuster
30. House R. & Loewenthal D. (editors) 2008. Against and For CBT: Towards a constructive dialogue. Ross-on-Wye: PCCS Books
31. House R. & Totton N. (editors) 1997. *Implausible Professions: Arguments for pluralism and autonomy in psychotherapy and counselling*. Ross-on-Wye: PCCS Books
32. Jeffers S. 1987. *Feel the Fear and Do It Anyway*. London: Century Hutchinson.
33. Jones D. (editor) 1994. *Innovative Therapy: A handbook*. Buckingham, PA: Open University Press.
34. Julian of Norwich edited by G. Warrack 1901 (originally

1373). *Revelations of Divine Love*. London: Methuen

35. Kierkegaard S. 1961. *Purity of Heart is to Wil One Thing*. New Your: Harper

36. Krech G. 2001. *Naikan: Gratitude, Grace and the Japanese Art of SelfReflection*. Berkeley, CA: Stone Bridge Press

37. Lawrence P. 1976. *Georg Simmel: Sociologist and European*. Sunbury-on-Thames, Middlesex: Nelson

38. Leijssen M. 1993. "Creating a Workable Distance to Overwhelming Images: Comments on a session transcript." In Brazier 1991, pp.129-147

39. Levant R.F. & Shlien J.M. (editors) 1984. *Client-Centered Therapy and The Person-Centered Approach: New Dirctions in Theory, Research and Practice*. Westport, CT: Praeger

40. Levitt B.E. (editor) 2005. *Embracing Non-directivity: Reassessing person-centered theory and practice in the 21st century*. Ross-on-Wye: PCCS Books

41. Lietaer G. Rombauts J. & Van Balen R (editors) 1990. *Client-Centered and Experiential Psychotherapy in the Nineties*. Leuven, Belgium: Leuven University Press

42. Lietaer G. 1990b. "The Client-Centered Approach after the Wisconsin Project: A personal view of its evolution". In Lietaer et al. 1990, pp.19-46.

43. Lilly J.C. 1973. *The Centre of the Cyclone*. New York: Bantam Books

44. Mair K.. 1997. "The Myth of Therapist Expertise" in House & Totton 1997, pp.87-98.

45. Maslow A.H. 1954. *Motivation and Personality*. New York: Harper

46. Menand L. 1987. *Discovering Modernism: T.S.Eliot and his Context*. Oxford: Oxford University Press

47. Midgley M. 2001. *Science and Poetry*. London: Routledge

48. Moreno J.L. 1934. *Who Shall Survive*. New York: Beacon House

49. Moreno J.L. 1977 *Psychodrama*. New York: Beacon House

50. Murdoch I. 1970. *The Sovereignty of Good*. London: Routledge & Kegan Paul

51. Murray G. 1964. *Humanist Essays*. London: George, Allen & Unwin

52. Nygren A. 1939. *Agape and Eros*. New York: Macmillan (2 volumes)

53. Padel R. 2007. *The Poem and the Journey*. London: Chatto & Windus

54. Pieper J. 1965. *Leisure the Basis of Culture*. London: Collins Fontana

55. Raskin N.J. 2005. "Historic Events in Cliet-Centered Therapy and the Person-Centered Approach". In Levitt 2005, pp.17-27.

56. Reich W. 1945/1972. *Character Analysis*. New York: Farrar, Straus & Giroux

57. Rogers C.R. 1939. *The Clinical Treatment of the Problem Child*. Boston: Houghton Mifflin

58. Rogers C.R. 1957. "The necessary and sufficient conditions of therapeutic personality change". *Journal of Consulting Psychology 21*, pp.95-103

59. Rogers C.R. 1961. *On Becoming a Person: A therapist's view of psychotherapy*. London: Constable

60. Rogers C.R. 1980. *A Way of Being*. Boston: Houghton Mifflin

61. Rogers C.R. 1983. *Freedom to Learn*. Columbus, Ohio: Charles E. Merrill

62. Rubin L.B. 1983. "Men, Women and Intimacy". In Soble 1989, pp.12-28

63. Scheff T.J. 1979/2001. *Catharsis in Healing, Ritual and Drama*. Lincoln NE: Authors Guild (originally University of California Press, 1979)

64. Shlien J.M. 1987. "A Countertheory of Transference" in *Person-Centered Review 2*. 1, February 1987

65. Shlien J.M. 1987b. "Further Thoughts on Transference" in *Person-Centered Review 2*. 4, November 1987

66. Shlien J.M. 2003. *To Lead an Honorable Life.* Ross-on-Wye: PCCS

67. Smail D. 1997. "Psychotherapy and Tragedy", in House & Totton 1997, pp.159-170.

68. Soble A. (editor) 1989. *Eros, Agape and Philia: Readings in the philosophy of love.* St Paul, Minnesota: Paragon.

69. Spinelli E. 1989. *The Interpreted World: An introduction to phenomenological psychology.* London: Sage

70. Stanton M. 1990. *Sandor Ferenczi: Reconsidering active intervention.* London: Free Association Books

71. Thorne B. 1992. *Carl Rogers.* London: Sage

72. Tocquevile A.de 1835/1945. *Democracy in America.* New York: Random House.

73. Trilling L. 1972. *Sincerity and Authenticity.* Cambridge MA: Harvard University Press

74. Van Belle H. 1990. "Rogers' Later Move Toward Mysticism: Implications for client-centered therapy". In Lietaer *et al.* 1990, pp.47-58.

75. Watson B. 1991. *Saigyo: Poems of a Mountain Home.* New York: Columbia University Press

76. Watts J. & Tomatsu Y. 2005. *Traversing the Pure Land Path: A lifetime of encounters with Honen Shonin.* Tokyo: Jodo Shu Press

77. Weinstein D. & Weinstei A.W. 1993. *Postmodern(ized) Simmel.* London: Routledge

78. CRR: The Carl Rogers Reader, edited by H. Kirschenbaum& V.L.Henderson. London: Constable 1990.

Glossary

Aesthetic Distance: Optimal distance (q.v.) as it applies in the arts. Aristotle suggested that optimally distanced drama induces catharsis (q.v.).

Agape: From Greek: Unconditional love, such as that of God or Buddha.

Amida Trust: The institute where David and Caroline Brazier developed the other centred approach situated at 12 Coventry Road, Narborough, Leicestershire, UK.
http://www.amidatrust.com

Buddha: The ideal person, according to the Buddhist tradition, being one who is free from conceit and so has fully woken up to the significance of the object world.

Catharsis: From Greek. Cleansing. The expression of emotion accompanying an experience of satisfaction, insight, remorse or completion that discharges an enduring tension that had built up that overly distanced a person from their object world.

Client Centred Therapy: The method of psychotherapy and counselling developed by Carl R. Rogers and described in his book of the same name published in 1951 in which the therapist's empathy for the client plays a central role.

Congruence: Genuineness. That condition in which one's outward expression matches one's inward state. In particular, in the theory of Carl Rogers, genuineness of positive regard (q.v.) and of empathy (q.v.).

Conserve: A term coined by Jacob Moreno to indicate those fixed or habitual elements in the psychology of an individual that reflect the culture in which he has lived.

Counselling: In general, counselling refers to any form of interpersonal helping that relies upon dialogue between counsellor and counsellee as its primary method. In the work of C.R.Rogers counselling refers to what is generally called psychotherapy.

Cultural Conserve: see Conserve.

Cultural Studies: The academic study of culture in all its aspects.

Carl R. Rogers (1902-1987): Humanistic psychologist and worker for international peace who developed a non-directive approach to psychotherapy subsequently developed into client centred therapy. When the principles of this method were later extended to education, groupwork, organization development and peace studies it was again renamed person centred approach.

Distance: As a technical term in psychology and in drama, refers to the emotional intensity with which a phenomenon is experienced which is a function both of the state of the observer and, more particularly, of the manner in which it is enacted or presented. A dramatic presentation or narrative can be over-distanced, in which case it is pallid; under-distanced, in which case it is alarming; or optimally distanced, in which case it is satisfying. See: Aesthetic Distance

Empathy: The ability to feel things in the manner of an other as if one were the other, yet without identification of oneself with that other.

Eros: From Greek: Love coloured by personal desire, including especially sexual desire.

Esteem: the felt value with which an object is regarded, especially when this value is positive.

Esteem Theory: Another name for other centred approach (q.v.)

Gegenwelt: From German. A term in existential philosophy denoting those aspects of the real world that one comes up against and that resist one's will. See also, Mitwelt, Umwelt.

Honen Shonin (1133-1212) Japanese Buddhist sage, renowned for his sanctity and understanding of the whole range of Buddhist teachings who nonetheless believed himself incapable of true virtue and founded the Pureland (Jodo) Sect upon principles of faith and humility.

Iris Murdoch (1919-1999): philosopher, novelist and playwright whose principle concerns were the nature of goodness, the sacred and taboo, and sexuality.

Jacob Moreno (1889-1974): Pioneer of psychotherapeutic method, especially in groups, existentialist, and proponent of experimental theatre. Founder of psychodrama, sociometry and sociodrama. He lived the first half of his life in Vienna and the second in New York.

Jessie Taft (1882-1960): anthropologist, social-interactionist, feminist, and biographer of Otto Rank (q.v.), she founded the Philadephia approach to social work and had a marked influence upon the early work of Carl Rogers (q.v.).

Julian of Norwich. Fourteenth century English anchoress. The first woman to publish a book in the English language. Known for her visions of Christ crucified that revealed to her the unconditionality of divine love.

Literary Criticism: That aspect of cultural studies that is concerned with the literary products of a culture including poetry, drama, fiction and other writing, and which concerns itself with questions of the quality and meaning of such work.

Martin Buber (1878-1965): Twentieth century Jewish theologian and existentialist philosopher whose ideas centre upon the primacy and modes of encounter between subject and object, person and God.

Mimesis: From Greek. Replication. A quality isolated by Aristotle as an essential hallmark of art.

Mitwelt: From German. A term in existential philosophy indicating the fantasy component of the object world (q.v.). The collection of significant others that a person carries with them as an internal audience or world to which they respond. See also Gegenwelt, Umwelt.

Naikan: From Japanese. Literally 'introspection' this actually refers to a method of therapy in which a person changes through close examination of the evidence of their life, especially of what they have received, what they have done in return and what trouble their existence has occasioned for others.

Nei Quan: From Chinese: see Naikan

Non-directive Therapy: The name given in the nineteen forties by C.R. Rogers (q.v.) to his method of counselling and psychotherapy that was subsequently renamed the client centred approach (q.v.)

Object: The object of consciousness including significant others whether human or otherwise.

Object World: The psychological environment of the person including both concrete realities and fantasy.

Oestrostasis: The tendency of an organism to attempt to maintain stability of stimulation level.

Other Centred Approach: The theory that the primary drive in human life is that of establishing a relationship of positive esteem with significant others elucidated in detail throughout this book.

Other Centred Therapy: The method of psychotherapy advanced in this book based upon esteem theory (q.v.)

Otto Rank (1884-1939): Viennese psychoanalyst and close associate of Freud who developed an empathic relational approach to psychotherapy. He placed considerable emphasis upon the importance of separation (one of love's inevitable disappointments) in pathology and character development. Through the work of Jessie Taft (q.v.) he was an influence upon Carl Rogers.

Optimal Distance: see: Distance, Aesthetic Distance

Over Distanced: see: Distance

Person Centred Approach: The name applied by C.R.Rogers to his method. The term Person Centred Approach was used when the ideas originally developed in client centred therapy (q.v.) were applied to spheres other than counselling such as education, management or peace studies.

Positive Regard: See: Unconditional Positive Regard.

Praxeis: From Greek. How things fare, faring, action and its consequence.

Psychotherapy: A form of counselling (q.v.) in which the intention is to facilitate change in the personality of the client or to bring about the over-coming of mental disease or malfunction.

Saigyo: Twelfth century Japanese Pureland Buddhist priest known as one of Japan's foremost poets. His works celebrate nature, loneliness, and spirituality often in an allusive or plaintive tone. They paved the way for a considerable widening of subject matter, realism, and new creativity in style in Japanese letters.

Sandor Ferenczi (1873-1933): Hungarian psychoanalyst who, in collaboration with Otto Rank (q.v.), developed an active empathic style of psychotherapeutic intervention. Like Rank saw a close relation between psychotherapy, literature and the arts.

T.S.Eliot (1888-1965): Poet, critic, editor and play-write who was one of the most influential figures in modern English letters. He was awarded the Nobel Prize for literature in 1948.

Umwelt: From German. A term in existential philosophy for those elements of the world that one is, as it were, programmed to respond to. See also, Mitwelt, Gegenwelt.

Unconditional Positive Regard: A term coined by Carl Rogers indicating a positive esteem held by a therapist for a client that is not conditional upon the client behaving or expressing himself in a particular way or conforming to other require-ments set by the therapist.

Under Distanced: see: Distance

Index

The terms love, frustration, esteem and disappointment, have not been indexed as they are the matter of the whole book. Please also see the Glossary on pages 181-185.

Internet Access to the Work of David & Caroline Brazier

http://www.amidatrust.com
http://amidatrust.ning.com
http://www.buddhistpsychology.info
http://www.othercentredapproach.com
http://www.infinities.info
http://amidatrust.typepad/dharmavidya
http://groups.to/poetrycircle/
http://profile.to/davidbrazier/

Also by David Brazier:

A Guide to Psychodrama
Beyond Carl Rogers
Zen Therapy
The Feeling Buddha
The New Buddhism
Who Loves Dies Well

& by Caroline Brazier

Buddhist Psychology
The Other Buddhism
Guilt
Listening to the Other
Other Centred Therapy

BOOKS

MySpiritRadio